Exchanging Lives

Exchanging Lives

Middle School Writers Online

Scott Christian
University of Alaska—Southeast

Foreword by

Andrea A. Lunsford
The Ohio State University

National Council of Teachers of English
1111 W. Kenyon Road, Urbana, Illinois 61801-1096

Prepress services: Precision Graphics

Staff Editor: Zarina M. Hock

Interior Design: Doug Burnett

Cover Design: Evelyn C. Shapiro

NCTE Stock Number: 16434-3050

Library of Congress Cataloging-in-Publication Data

Christian, Scott, 1962–
    Exchanging lives : middle school writers online / Scott Christian;
foreword by Andrea A. Lunsford.
      p.   cm.
    Includes bibliographical references (p.) and index.
    ISBN 0-8141-1643-4 (pbk.)
    1. Anne Frank Conference (Online writers project)   2. English
language--Composition and exercises--Study and teaching (Middle
school)--United States--Data processing.   I. Title.
LB1631.C4495   1997
808'.042'0712--dc21
                                                       97-23713
                                                            CIP

Contents

Acknowledgments

I would like to thank the entire community of the Bread Loaf School of English for their vigorous support of rural education in general and projects like this book. James Maddox, Director; Dixie Goswami, Coordinator of the Bread Loaf Rural Teacher Network (BLRTN); Rocky Gooch, Director of Telecommunications; Caroline Eisner, Technical Consultant; and Elaine Hall, Administrative Assistant, have provided the vision and the nuts-and-bolts support for teachers to consider and to implement systemic change in their classrooms and schools. Carla Asher, program officer for the DeWitt Wallace/Reader's Digest Fund (the central funding agent of the BLRTN), deserves recognition for the wisdom to see the power in bringing teachers together in a way that had never been attempted.

My heartfelt thanks to all the teachers in the BLRTN and especially to those involved in the first three years of the Anne Frank Conference, on which this book is based: Tom McKenna, Mary Burnham, Peggy Turner, Sondra Porter, Phillip Sittnick, Helena Fagan, Les Fortier, and Patricia Parrish. Thanks also to all the students who have participated in the Anne Frank Conference, including those whose writing is presented here. Specifically, I'd like to thank Theresa and Holly Petty, Annabeth Miller, Shauntae Steward, Joel Gennari, Jenny Anderson, and all my students at Nikiski Middle School for teaching their teacher about writing and literature. My colleagues and friends at Nikiski Middle School, Lori Manion and Ward Romans, deserve thanks for their constant support and encouragement during the long and often mysterious process that has resulted in this book.

Thank you to Michael Greer, the wise, professional, and always focused editor, and to everyone at the National Council of Teachers of English for making this book happen.

There are people in our lives whose influence is so dramatic, so sudden yet long-lasting, that it is difficult to imagine ourselves before we knew them. Andrea Lunsford and Dixie Goswami, two of the finest teachers and writers anywhere, have given selflessly for many years to teachers like me, who try to make sense of their learning through writing—a difficult and messy business. For these two leaders, visionaries and people of infinite kindness and patience, I can only offer my sincere thank you.

Thanks, as always, to my wife, Jeoung, and my children, Hannah and Paul, for your constant support, encouragement, and flexibility. You are the center of my universe.

Foreword

Several years ago, I sat with Scott Christian on a porch at the Bread Loaf School of English in the lush Green Mountains of Vermont, puzzling and fussing over reams of transcripts gleaned from an online conference he and colleagues and students from Alaska, Mississippi, Vermont, and New Mexico had conducted during the school year. Even then, as we struggled to make sense of this vast patchwork quilt of a conversation, I sensed the power of this exchange, heard the student's voices reaching out across the wires, across divides of place, culture, race, and age. How fortunate I felt to have met Scott and the other remarkable and talented teachers pursuing M.A. and M.Litt. degrees in Bread Loaf's rigorous and innovative program; how lucky we all were to be working with Jim Maddox, Dixie Goswami, and the other distinguished scholars and researchers who make up the Bread Loaf faculty; how absolutely blessed we were to be linked through BreadNet, arguably the largest and certainly the most successful teacher telecommunications network in the country. And how much I looked forward to following Scott's work on this project, both online and—I hoped—in person.

Now I am again enjoying Scott Christian's company. Flying home from a meeting on the West Coast, I finish reading the draft of *Exchanging Lives* and look down at the mountains and plains passing beneath me, the land across which leap the conversations of middle- and high-school students from the four corners of our country. I hear Annabeth, whose response to *Anne Frank: Diary of a Young Girl* opens this book. And I hear Shauntae, Jenny, Monika, Brad, and Nikki—their growing engagement with Anne Frank, with the power of writing, and with each other. I hear, too, the voices of other teacher/scholars—Peggy Turner from Guntown, Mississippi; Phil Sittnick from Laguna, New Mexico; Mary Burnham from Newbury, Vermont. Most of all, I hear Alaskan Scott Christian's clearheaded, warm, and witty voice guiding readers—with the teacher's eye for the "small, good things" that occur daily in our classrooms—through the online exchanges that, as he says, "forever altered my understandings of literacy."

In taking this journey toward new understandings, Scott brilliantly evokes the teacherly life at his middle school in Nikiski; leads readers through the increasingly rich, complex conversations among his students and those at the other far-flung school sites that make up the Anne Frank Conference; pauses to reflect intensely on one student's experience online; and draws out the implications of this conference and other networking activities for teachers and students working for real educational change in a richly diverse world. As Scott's study of the Anne Frank Conference demonstrates, deeply collaborative online exchanges like this one hold out strong promise of changing ways of writing, certainly—but attitudes and lives as well. As students move toward the kind of "striving writing" that seeks to connect with an audience in particularly thought-provoking ways, or to the "talking writing" that Scott sees emerging in intense online dialogues, they show—more powerfully than can any dozen books on technology and education—how networked conversations can bring literature to life and use it to illustrate and enrich the lives of students coming from vastly different places.

In an address to teachers of reading and writing, Jacqueline Jones Royster asks, "How can we teach, engage in research, write about and talk across boundaries with others, instead of for, about, and around others?" Scott Christian's *Exchanging Lives* offers one compelling answer to these questions. Read on. Meet the students and teachers at work here. Listen closely to them. And pass their messages on.

Andrea A. Lunsford

Introduction

In order to teach writing, we have to continually seek and find writing in our classrooms that is honest, spirited, and reasoned, and that informs us as people. Annabeth Miller's essay exemplifies what I'm after in the language arts classroom. This is what it's all about. It is my contention that online literary exchanges, like the Anne Frank Conference, which will be the focus of this book, result in a much greater understanding of the literary text. And, because the students are writing to other students in other parts of the country, not merely to the teacher or to the students sitting beside them, they have an opportunity to create a new self, an online version of themselves as students and people. This opportunity raises the level of concern about their writing, which leads to better, more effective writing. Annabeth's essay, "Growing Up," is an example of what I seek most in the literature classroom, a student using her life experience as a means to better understand, to "read" the book, and then to use this exercise to "read" her life as well. Annabeth wrote a few paragraphs in her response journal about how Anne was growing up in the novel. I wrote back a couple of questions and asked her to think about her writing and the book again. She came in the next day with a draft of the essay that was very close to this final version.

Growing Up
Annabeth Miller

Growing up is really hard to do, not physically, but emotionally. When you're growing up, you go through many changes. You notice and do things that you've never noticed or done before. All of a sudden you start fighting with your family members, trying their patience, or arguing at every chance you get. You also start to discover and understand things like prejudice, responsibilities, and life in general.

Just like everyone else, Anne Frank went through these changes. At the beginning of the diary, I don't think Anne really understood herself. At times she thought a great deal of herself. I, too, once thought highly of myself, not for very long, but long enough to understand that I am no better than anyone else. But we all do have some qualities about ourselves that we should be proud of. As time went on, Anne didn't write in the diary about herself as much as she had in the beginning. She started to understand what I, too, had to understand.

Anne started to notice things she never noticed before, let alone even cared about. For example, when Peter first came to the Secret Annex, Anne probably took one look at him and classified him as gawky and obviously a "nerd." But, as she grew older, she started to look on the inside of him. She discovered he was kind, gentle, and had a great attitude. Therefore, she "fell in love" with him. Anne discovered exactly what the saying "A book can't be judged by its cover" meant. She understood that on the inside of people, they could be a whole different person.

Anne didn't really seem to care much about other people's feelings when she was young. She was going through a rough time when she came to realize this about herself. Once, when her dad didn't come up to her room to pray with her, her mother decided that she would. That was a nice and caring thing her mother tried to do, but when she got up there, Anne told her to go away and that she didn't want her to pray with her. Her mother started crying and ran out of the room. That was really cold of Anne to do to her mother. After all, she was just trying to help. Anne thought about it, and realized that was an awful thing she had done.

Anne found that she didn't like the way she felt after she told her mother that. She began to discover and learn about other people's feelings. After this, Anne looked on the inside of people and tried to understand their feelings. Once, when I was younger, I got really mad at my mom and told her I hated her. When I remembered how much it hurt me when my sisters said that to me, I regretted saying it to my mom. When I realized how much I hurt her, I felt terrible. I really didn't hate her, but sometimes my mouth just outruns my head. Now I try not to say or think those kind of things to anybody, no matter how much they hurt me or how mad I am at them. And, I try not to say anything to anyone that might hurt their feelings.

Anne really was a great girl. By the time she was fourteen, she was kind, smart, caring and she had lost all of her old babyish ways. When Anne was taken to the concentration camp, the kindness in her heart really began to show. As she watched the people around her pass away, she still worked on keeping her hopes up. As she watched the gypsy children being taken off to the gas chambers, she looked in their eyes and saw all the pain, sorrow, and suffering. That would be the hardest thing to do. When she passed away, I believe her very mature spirit was still in the hearts of all of her friends who knew her.

As you can see, Anne grew up from a selfish, noncaring little girl into a bright, cheery, hopeful young woman. Anne is a hero to many people of all different colors, religions, and countries. She is admired for her understanding and sensitivity to those around her.

Annabeth was in eighth grade when she wrote the preceding essay. At this level, there is a broad spectrum of writing skills and abilities. When it comes to expository writing, there are some students who have extreme difficulty staying with one idea for any length of time, and other students who are writing very sophisticated pieces. When Annabeth handed this to me, I was stunned. I had never seen a piece of writing quite like this from an eighth grader. Not only had she kept her purpose in focus, she had used relevant, personal experiences and impressions to make her writing come alive. When I posted this essay online toward the end of the Anne Frank Conference, there were many kind responses from around the network, including a personal note from Jim Maddox, the Director of the Bread Loaf School of English. Annabeth received a great deal of praise in our school as well, as I shared her writing with all my classes, and the high school English teacher did the same. Teaching writing, at its most basic, is like agriculture: we can do our very best to prepare the field, to plant the seed, to nurture the plants, but there is much that is out of our control. However, we can learn from each crop how best to seek the highest yield, and online literary exchanges are a fertile field for nurturing strong young writers.

The Anne Frank Conference, an online literary exchange among middle school students, has been in existence since early 1993. In the first three years of its existence (the time frame of this book), more than eight hundred students read the Anne Frank diary and discussed their views, as well as just about everything in their lives, online. For many students like Annabeth, that experience has fundamentally changed who they are as writers. And for us, as teachers with widely disparate teaching experiences, watching these conferences unfold and take on their own energy and direction has been transformational in our views of teaching literature and writing.

In this book, which began as a teacher research project to examine the original transcript of the first conference, we will go inside the Anne Frank Conference to try to make sense of this new phenomenon in education. Just as we do in class before we read the diary, we will set the stage by "going to" Europe just prior to World War II by reading magazine articles, viewing movies, and researching various aspects of the historical period in the library. Next, we'll go into my classroom so that we can get a sense of how this methodology fits into a teaching practice. Then we're off into the world of the Anne Frank Conference. I'll begin with a structured view of the nuts and bolts of the exchange and place it in the context of the classrooms involved. Next, we'll look closely at the writing itself, using a taxonomy I've developed to better understand this new literacy which is emerging. We'll also hear Jenny Anderson's story of her experience as a student participant in the Anne Frank Conference this past school year. Lastly, I'll discuss some of the implications of the exchange in terms of the literacy of our students and ourselves as teachers.

In the fall of 1992—just before the events described in this book had begun—I had a nagging sense that I was missing the boat in one area: I knew that a lot of my students' writing wasn't genuine, thoughtful, sincere work. After a lot of experimentation on my part, and discussion with other teachers, I felt that there were no huge new areas of pedagogy to explore. I was beginning to resign myself to the fact that our school system was producing a culture of "typers," word assemblers, and page fillers, instead of writers. I was beginning to think that the students who did invest in their writing were the nonconformists, who bucked the system, determined to become writers despite the system. The longer I teach, I find it easier and easier to join the blame game in our profession. It is the parents who don't read to their kids. It is the television, the elementary schools, the lack of physical exercise, the depletion of the ozone, the liberal media, and "the culture of irresponsibility and victimization" that the conservatives have found as scapegoats, or the lack of blue algae in our diet that are to blame for the lack of intrinsic motivation to learn. If you want to, there are all kinds of ways to explain why kids aren't performing the way we'd like them to. Of course the most difficult task is accepting the blame ourselves. Looking back, I see that although I was doing a lot of things right a critical component was missing from my classroom.

I don't want to paint a bleak picture here. There were many good things happening in our middle school: interdisciplinary teaching, quality student publications, cooperative learning activities, and portfolio assessment. We had created a positive learning environment and a community of reflective learners. Still, I knew there had to be a way to generate more quality writing from the students. I didn't make a conscious decision to explore online literary exchanges as a medium for addressing this deficiency. But, as I do with all new approaches and materials that come my way, I ran the concept through the blender of my teaching philosophy: Is it student centered? Is it open-ended? Is there room for collaboration? Is it process oriented? Is it flexible enough to allow for differences between classrooms, students, teachers? Is it equitable for diverse classrooms and students? How will this impact the structure of my classroom? Will it be *boring* for me or my students? These aren't just buzzwords and catch phrases. As a runner, I don't sign up for a race unless it fits into my training program. As a parent, I don't take my kids to a movie or to a play unless I think it is appropriate developmentally. Likewise, I don't hop into something with my students unless I think it meets these criteria. In the end, I had an intuitive sense that an online literary exchange would be a worthwhile project and perhaps an adventure, or at least a great learning experience, even though I had no clue that it would unleash the kinds of writing that exploded across the wires over the next three years.

It needs to be said emphatically that I am not a "technology teacher." I don't have the last ten issues of *MacWorld* in a drawer in my desk, and I can't explain to you the intricacies of how a motherboard works, or even how messages are sent and received through phone wires. I have always been on a strictly "need-to-know" basis with technology. At best, this relationship has been a peaceful coexistence. If there is something I need to do with technology as a teacher, a researcher, a writer, or a parent, or if there is a task that I'd like my students to perform, I will seek out the information and training that I need. But it is only a means to an end. I view technology as a cumbersome, time-consuming, expensive, but very necessary and enriching tool in my profession. Put simply, if I could generate the kind of student writing and enthusiasm that happened in the Anne Frank Conference without telecommunications, I'd do it. Thankfully, the technology part was very simple, allowing us techno-neophytes to hop in and ride with the pros.

As a teacher (and a student), I've always resisted authority and enjoyed the pursuit of doing things my way. One of the things that I like about teaching is that I have profound influence over what happens within that sphere. But it is also this ownership and freedom which give us that nagging sense of guilt when we hear about something exciting, supposedly the next wave in education, and we're not riding it. So, when I read about surfing the net and students conversing with astronauts at NASA, sending e-mail to the president, and talking about earthquakes with survivors in Mexico, I knew I had to check it out. I couldn't just walk in and ask my administrator for help connecting to the Internet (as if he'd be willing or able to help, anyway). I had to find a way that made sense for my students and me. To be honest, I had to find the support to experiment with this technology without disappointing my students or wasting valuable time in the classroom.

Before attending the Bread Loaf School of English, I had never done more than e-mail in terms of telecommunications. I had seen Netscape and color images of cities around the world on a friend's computer, but that was it. Obviously, I wasn't a techno-whiz kid out looking for a hot new project to test my prowess. The best analogy I could make for what happened at Bread Loaf would be going into the bookstore looking for a gift for a friend, abandoning that search, and finding a novel that fundamentally changes your outlook on life. *It is in the pursuit and recognition of wondrous, spectacular accidents that we grow as teachers.* Connecting five classrooms in an online literary exchange, and discovering the impact on my students' literacy, was this sort of accident.

Among other insights into my students' lives, along with literacy, collaboration with other teachers, and adolescents in general, I discovered that literary exchanges through telecommunications are a critical tool in successful pedagogy. In these exchanges students take more risks as writers, experimenting with language, style, vocabulary, and literary devices. The level of concern became greater in their writing because the writing had a real purpose and a genuine audience who read and responded to the writing. Students became excited about reading, discussing, and writing about literature, which led them to become more critical and thoughtful readers. The exchanges were a catalyst for developing a sense of community within the classroom, as students discussed the similarities and differences of the lifestyles and points of view of students from other regions of the country.

Above all, this book is about students making sense of their world, their lives, and a work of literature through writing. It follows, then, that the student writing in the book is the anchor, the focus, and the driving force in the conversation about teaching and learning.

1 Teacher as Learner

As a middle school teacher, I have grown weary of the jokes that adolescence is a disease that fortunately isn't fatal; that instead of middle school, teenagers should be sent to distant islands to work in the fields until they grow up; and so on. I have to take a breath when I'm on a plane or at a meeting, or visiting relatives, and I mention that I teach eighth grade; the responses range from dismay to disparaging comments about how kids at this age "aren't even human." For me, there is no other age that I would prefer to teach. If anything, it is at this age when kids are *most* human. In the middle-school language arts classroom, the opinionated, argumentative, emotional, energetic, curious, sometimes reckless spirit of young adults creates the kind of energy and dynamic tension that, for me, is the impetus for being a teacher. This is a trying time for young adults, but there is no better place to grapple with the confusion of becoming, and leaving childhood behind, than in the experiencing of literature: the reading, thinking, discussing, and writing about other lives that are brought into our own, and growing vicariously through others' living.

After teaching for eight years in a variety of settings, I felt fairly confident in the language arts classroom. I had experimented with various pedagogies: response journals, reading and writing workshops, student anthologies, Socratic seminars, and others. Even though for every step forward there was a world of questions about how I might do things differently, or better, I felt that when kids left my room they generally had more confidence as readers, writers, and speakers, and that they were more proficient and skilled in these areas. Nevertheless, I always had a nagging sense that I was missing the boat in terms of releasing the genuine adolescent voice in their writing.

From time to time, in response journals I would hear the oddball humor, the sometimes dark, pessimistic view of the world, the genuine heartfelt angst, and the confusion that is typical of adolescents. Yet, to be honest, the writing often was "to the teacher" in tone, style, and content. Students would go through the motions of getting their thoughts on paper, and would superficially make connections between the texts and their lives, because that was expected in the journals and discussions. In the response journals I would sometimes develop a dialogue with the student in which the talk would become genuine and purposeful, and I could sense that the writer was making a sincere effort to write thoughtfully.

In a teacher research project a few years ago, I looked closely at these responses and found there was often a private self presented in the journals, different from the public self displayed in the classroom. The pressure of fitting in with peers often caused students to create a personality for the classroom, different from the real, often more mature self presented in their journals. Through these journals, in which (at my request) kids not only wrote about reading, but examined their processes as writers as well, I also learned about how students selected topics and their attitudes toward writing. The wide variation in the individual differences in their writing processes was a revelation. There were frequent entries about students' perceptions of publishing and their real perceptions of their own and other students' writing. I found the journals to be a window into what really happened (or didn't) during peer response conferences. The response journals were also a forum for frequently asked questions about writing. Despite this step forward in my learning as a writing teacher, I was still longing to release the deluge of emotions, questions, voices, and energy which I knew was just under the surface of my students' often perfunctory, teacher-driven writing. Although there is no panacea in our challenging profession, my experience with the Anne Frank Conference shed important light on what needs to be in place for kids to write from the heart, to care about the words they place on the paper.

I felt part of my frustration not only as a teacher but as a writer as well. I originally came to Alaska to teach for one year in order to save money to support myself while I completed the revision of a novel I had written as an undergraduate. William Kittredge, a fabulous writing teacher at the University of Montana, had spent hours with me, one-on-one in his office, guiding me toward finding structure and developing a voice which would sustain the reader through the narrative. Although my novel was, in his words, "sometimes brilliant, and sometimes, certainly not," I did have a great big stack of typed paper on my desk, and it was thrilling. I thrived on the power of coming home from classes and my part-time job at a drugstore and creating a world, moving people through that world, seeing them change and grow, and becoming omnipotent through writing. I also loved to write bad poetry, and I kept journals and wrote letters. Although I think the romantic idea of the writing life was a motivator as well, I have always had a passion for creating, for putting words on paper, for the adrenaline rush of thinking that the words are good and will be read and considered. Although I certainly do not have a passion for revision, the writing itself is a joy for me. Although I was surprised by the rewards and the compelling nature of teaching and decided to stick with it for a while (eleven years now and counting), I still consider myself a writer, and I want desperately for my students to unleash the power of creating worlds and ideas through writing. I know that everyone isn't going to enjoy the creative moment the way that I do, but unless they get past the drudgery of page filling and rote, mindless exercises of word assembling, they won't experience the *joy* of writing.

I'm also not embarrassed to admit that I enjoyed writing analytically for my literature classes as an English major. Through the writing process, the discussions, and the experimentations and intuitions that are critical to that process, I would inevitably learn something relevant about myself and the world we live in. It is growing increasingly unpopular, and even clichéd these days to talk about the effect of literature on our lives. With all of the buzz about tech prep and standards and learning outcomes, teaching literature can become an afterthought. As Mem Fox describes in her wonderful book, *Radical Reflections*, I am determined that my classroom not be a desert.

> We need to water the desert so that the writing will bloom. By *watering the desert* I mean providing children with the most wonderful literature available: the classics, the new, the beautiful, the revolting, the hysterical, the puzzling, the amazing, the riveting. We need to fill their storehouses with events, characters, styles, emotions, places, and themes that will help them to grow, not wither, thirsty in the desert of illiteracy. (p. 67)

> Margot and mummy's natures are completely strange to me. I can understand my friends better than my own mother—too bad!
>
> *Anne Frank: The Diary of a Young Girl*
> Sunday, September 27th, 1942.

Although adolescence is a troubling time, when the actions of adults—particularly parents and teachers—seem mystifying, the difficulty of growing through the experience unites young people and cements the connections they make with one another. After reading Anne Frank, most of my eighth-grade students agreed vigorously with Anne: their friends made infinitely more sense of the world than did their parents. This unique quality of adolescents, the tendency to form strong bonds and to delight in connections with their peers, creates dynamic communication in the classroom. Students at all ages have friends and form relationships with their peers. However, between the approximate ages of eleven to fourteen, these relationships are the single most important consideration in their lives. (As a friend of mine once pointed out, *whom* an eighth grader sits next to in class is much more important to that student than *what* is going on at the front of the classroom.) I think this was one of the factors for the strong momentum that developed within the Anne Frank Conference.

Teaching literature and writing is about connecting: the exchanging, the examining, and the growing of lives, both on the page and in our classrooms. As soon as the project known as the Anne Frank Conference began, the teachers involved sensed that this would be something very different for everyone. I've learned that in order to be successful in the classroom, I have to attempt to put myself in the place of my students, to reflect on my own experience and to anticipate theirs. Although this is often a haphazard and wishful task at best, the process is worthwhile. To begin the Anne Frank Conference, I wrote the following letter to my students.

12-21-92
Dear Students,

It is a windy, cold afternoon as I write to you. Yesterday the spruce trees outside my window were heavily weighted by the recent wet snow. But today the snow has blown away and the spruce rock back and forth, like a choir that is oddly out of rhythm. As I sit down to write, I am thinking about you, about being thirteen, and about our new quest before us.

As you know, it is my first year with the Bulldogs. I transferred here so that I could teach language arts again, something that I love to do. I have been pleasantly surprised by the one feature of this school that sets it apart from any school that I have attended as a student, worked in as a teacher, or visited in my travels. Here, students tolerate the uniqueness of each other. I won't say that you celebrate the individuality of others regularly, although it does happen. But you respect differing views and styles and likes and dislikes. Sometimes there is cruelty, as in any situation where humans spend a lot of time together, but it is rare. I thank you for that. In the classroom, if people aren't comfortable enough with themselves, they certainly won't take the risk of sharing their opinions, thoughts, and writing. When we shared our autobiographical writing and assembled the projects, I was amazed by the honesty and power of your stories. I know that it was stressful to get it all done and put it all together, but didn't it feel good to have a reflection of yourself, of your family, to keep forever?

I think the most heartwarming example of this openness was when we read the passage in Theresa's "Hungry Heart" about Serena dying of anorexia. This was not an easy thing to read about, to think about, to write about. Yet, you handled this delicate subject, and this brave move on Theresa's part, like mature adults. Early one morning, as I read your responses to this story, I was reminded again by how difficult it is to be a teenager, in this or at any time. Although I frequently nag you as a class about the horrors of homonyms, the idea of quality writing over quantity, and the importance of deadlines, you're a fine group of bright young people. Now that we've had some time to get to know each other, it is time to take down the walls, to push the zones of comfort that surround all of us, and to take on some fundamental ideas about living. I think we're ready.

I turned thirteen in the summer of 1976. At that time, our country was trying to recover from the darkness of Watergate and Vietnam by a grand, patriotic celebration of our two-hundredth birthday. For me, an eighth grader at Jefferson Junior High, in Naperville, Illinois, it was truly the best of times and the worst of times. On one hand, I had finally succeeded in making the "A" team on our local swim club, a group that traveled to the state capital for the championship. A friend and I had just completed our collection of all fifty 7-Up cans that, when turned in the correct order, created the image of Uncle Sam. We must have dug through a hundred dumpsters trying to find the cans with Idaho and Nevada on the back. It had also been a good year in school; my grades weren't great, but I wasn't grounded, either. My first girlfriend and I were going to the weekly "Junior High Jinx" at the YMCA, where we'd steal kisses during the cartoons upstairs. But, like I said, there was a dark side, too. My parents weren't getting along very well. My onetime hero, former President Richard Nixon, had resigned in disgrace. We were just pulling out of the oil crisis, which kept my dad from driving our new 1975 GMC Suburban with the 455 engine. My best friend had just moved to North Carolina, and high school, at Naperville North (student population 2,700) loomed ominously in the fall.

It was late in the spring when we read *The Diary of Anne Frank*. At the time, I had great difficulty separating Sharon Reice, the girl of my dreams, from characters in literature, or anything else in my life for that matter. She used to pass notes through various couriers two or three times each day. Interestingly, I think many of you learned to fold your notes in the same intricate and difficult patterns that Sharon pioneered. The highlight of each school day was when all the couples would sit together and the boys would very ceremoniously empty the cafeteria trays for the girls and, when we could, buy them an ice cream sandwich. If the planets were aligned just so, and we had managed to avoid the epidemic of jealousy that could be ignited by what were to us truly mysterious origins, we could then sit underneath the willows on the playground and alternately hold hands and throw grass and twigs at each other. I have heard that your romances of the nineties are a great deal more sophisticated, but you have to remember that this was way back in the seventies.

As I mentioned, we were reading a serious work of literature. Mrs. Johanns, who pronounced literature as if it had about nineteen syllables, would read an entry or two from the book to us every afternoon. We were then assigned to read a few entries on our own. It was during this time that I would hold my book dutifully in front of me, while I plotted a way to sneak over to Sharon's basketball practice after school, or a way to weasel a few dollars of ice cream money from my folks, or whatever. For some reason, I always had extreme difficulty reading in school. I liked to take my books home, sit on my bed, put on WLS quietly (so my beastly sister wouldn't scream through the walls), and read. At the time, "Philadelphia Freedom," by Elton John, and everything ever performed by The Who was the rage. I remember sitting on my bed and innocently turning to the back of the book. It was there that I read that Anne Frank had died in a concentration camp. Mrs. Johanns hadn't told us that.

We just assumed that, since her diaries made it through the occupation and the war, she had survived. I clearly remember going to school the next day, thinking about Sharon Reice in a concentration camp. It was one of the most frightening ideas that had ever occurred to me. I don't know about you, but when I was thirteen, the idea of death was a very serious business. When I read about Anne Frank, even though it had happened in Germany more than thirty years before, it made me realize that we were all mortal. Considering everything that was happening in my life at that time, it didn't exactly improve my outlook.

But now, when I look back, and as I read the book again this last month, the magic of literature warms my heart. Over and over, I've heard students ask, "Why do we have to read this?" I, too, asked that question, as recently as this past summer when I was back in school. I want to tell you that the answer is: because of the voices in the books and what they have to say about our lives. Anne Frank will soon be talking to us about her parents, her school, her home, her memories, her first boyfriend, her hometown and the horrible, difficult time when she was alive. As we are listening to her, take time to think about these aspects of your own life, to compare, to reflect, to discover how *you* feel about these things. I'm not going to ask you to like this book, or to be entertained by it. I'm asking you to listen to Anne, as if she were a new student in our class for a few months.

We won't be alone. There are students in other classes in Alaska, Vermont, and Missisippi who will be reading the book at the same time. We will be listening to these students and their thoughts and reactions to the book as well. Like the students from other states, we will be writing and sending our ideas to them, through telecommunications. As I mentioned at the beginning of this letter, you, as a group of people, have been very accepting of each other.

Let's welcome Anne Frank into our classroom and listen to what she has to say.

Sincerely,
Mr. C.

The reactions to the letter were mixed. As I read it aloud, there were giggles during the "stealing kisses" line and a few yawns here and there. As a whole, though, I think the kids were interested in the letter. For eighth-grade students, the single most important ingredient in establishing a productive and positive community of writers is that they relate to the teacher as a human being. Unless they view the teacher as a real person, instead of an alien from a strangely literate planet where all that is done is reading and writing, the teacher has no credibility. This letter was an attempt to further establish myself as a person in my students' eyes and to set the stage for the reading and writing that would take place in the Anne Frank Conference. I also wanted to demonstrate my joy for writing. I had written this letter because I wanted to, because I wanted to express some ideas that were important to me, not because it was an assignment or a requirement for employment. Mem Fox, a wonderful example of teacher as learner, puts it this way:

By attempting to be creative ourselves as teachers and users of language, we give our students not only a demonstration of teaching options but also the permission to use those creative options themselves. We demonstrate that effective learning and teaching are rarely based on chalk-and-talk. (p. 29)

As a writer, I continually use writing as a means to understand myself and the world around me. After returning from Bread Loaf my first summer, and prior to the start of the Anne Frank Conference, I sat down after a long run and had a go at getting my thoughts about the four main roles in my life—father, husband, teacher, runner—into some assemblage of order, to try to see how they were or weren't fitting together. I'd like to offer an excerpt from that personal writing before we begin our discussion of the online literacy exchange, just as I always like to talk with my students a bit about things other than writing to have a sense of who they are before we start a writing conference. One of the reasons that I resist the grand proclamations, sweeping generalizations, and quantitative analysis of university research in education is that there is often little context provided. The great advantage of teacher- or practitioner-initiated research is that a teacher can at least attempt to describe some of the countless variables that effect learning in the classrooms. Although I originally wrote the following narrative as a journal entry, I offer it here, slightly revised, in order to provide a setting for the online literary exchange and a more intimate picture of the students and the classroom in which the Anne Frank Conference first developed.

A Day in the Life

Teaching is my connection to the world. It keeps me grounded through contact with the bright young minds of my students, and the continual exchange of ideas. For a while, I wanted to be a writer. I still think that a time will come when that is how I spend a larger portion of my days. But for now, I find myself engaged in one of the most fascinating, rewarding, frustrating, exhilarating jobs that is available in our society. Keep in mind that this is one day. Out of the approximately sixteen hundred days that I've spent in the classroom, no two have been alike.

First hour is like a haven for wayward teachers. There is no way that a teacher could spend much time with these ninth graders without falling in love with them. As the kids would say, they are "way cool, rad, awesome" and, yes, "sweet!" If all of my classes were like this one, I would teach until I died and then would volunteer for a few more years after that (as some of my past colleagues have done). Today we are reading Juliet's soliloquy in act 3, scene 2. There was a time when I worried about the number of books that were "done." Now, I am much more concerned with quality learning than with quantity. Upstairs during my quiet time, I had decided to ask for a written response. I wrote two questions on the board: What do you think of Romeo and Juliet and their relationship? What is the root cause of the problem in the play? Now, English teachers have come under fire in the writings of people like Patrick Diaz for teaching an "answer" to literature. Critics claim that by suggesting that there is only one way to correctly respond to a work of literature, teachers are stifling students' views of it. I agree; however, I don't think we need to withdraw completely from the scene. I put the questions on the board and ask the students to open their books and complete a five-minute free write. As usually happens, several students crank out a paragraph in about two minutes, several are still rubbing sleep from their eyes, a few are staring at the board as if an answer will magically appear, and some are leafing through their books. Just as the five minutes are up, most have at least begun to write. I will spare you the details of their response training. Suffice it to say that most are now fairly comfortable with trying out their ideas on paper.

We then sort of float for a while, some students writing, some not, until it seems like most of the kids are ready to talk. I ask them to share their ideas, either from their writing or something that occurred to them while writing, or after. One girl asks very seriously, "What is the difference between lust and love?" There are several replies, like "Love is more painful," "Love is when you're willing to risk things for someone else," "Love only happens after lust," and so on. One of my dear students mentions the difference between Romeo's feelings for Rosaline compared to his feelings for Juliet. Then the same girl asks, "How do you know when you're in love?" A boy very authoritatively says, "It takes at least eight months, trust me." We then move on, trying to define the word in different contexts—the love of hamburgers versus the love of a child or the love of a lover, and so on.

We never reach a tangible conclusion to the discussion. Instead, these thoughts and opinions become a new part of our shared history, the foundation of future discussions. It is these often open-ended, meandering explorations of the text that help to form the foundation of our community, from which we draw the seeds of writing, both formally and informally. Like a photographer switching lenses and angles and exposures, we sit in a circle and experiment with words. It is, quite simply, a good serious talk about things that matter. This is why I am in my profession. I think it is important to do this with young people—not to give the answers, nor even provide the questions that are addressed (as in this instance), but to provide the forum, to assist in creating a community where ideas and opinions and questions are valued. Until this year I hadn't taught high school students since my first two years as a teacher. I felt horribly inadequate at that time. Perhaps it was because I was only twenty-two, and was separated from my senior students by only a few years and a million miles of culture. (My first year of teaching was in a Yup'ik village where English was a second language.) Now, although I love the energy of the middle school students, I do like the willingness of the high school students, at least this group of ninth graders, to admit that they are unsure of themselves about important issues. Eighth graders are so concerned with convincing everyone (including themselves) that they are mature and sophisticated, they sometimes avoid that openness, that risk taking.

First hour, as usual, was a wonderful time. I don't like to see those kids leave the room. Sometimes I want to keep them, or take them somewhere, or just thank them. And I do thank them, and I tell them that I like them and that I enjoy spending time with them and reading their writing. We have to love our students, even when it can be hard to like them.

Second hour is very different. It is my most challenging class, the result of "arena scheduling," a system in which the students parade from teacher to teacher when signing up for classes. I've never seen the perfect system for scheduling, and the fact that we are a junior/senior high with teachers who cross over makes the master schedule quite a challenge. There are two things I don't like about this scheduling system. One, it occasionally forces me to tell a student that he or she is not welcome in my classroom; sometimes this is my initial contact with the student. If I don't control the registration I can end up with fifty students in one section and none in another. Oddly enough, this did happen to some degree anyway. Secondly, the system allows groups of students to register for classes with their buddies. Now I am a strong believer in cooperative learning and I want kids to be happy in school, but I was once thirteen also. I remember a math class in particular where I had landed with several of my good buddies on the swim team. We were not juvenile delinquents individually, but, as a group, we were consistently disruptive. I remember one instance when the teacher suggested that we start our own construction company, because we were so good at throwing up roadblocks and erecting detours. I think if class scheduling were done by computer (and we do have the software), it would avoid both of these situations. My point in all of this is quite simple. I have a group of girls who shouldn't be in the same class together, and a group of boys who probably should not be in the same building together. They are not bad kids (my mantra as I enter the room). The problem is their collective consciousness, or the disintegration of it, which renders them difficult to deal with at times.

On this day, Thursday, we start in my classroom. For this class and this class only, there are specific instructions on the board, designed to prepare the students to be productive in the computer lab upstairs. I've already learned that once they are there, and the computers are on, it would take at least five hundred decibels of teacher volume to adjust their behavior as a group. We read the board together: Everyone will bring their writing and disks with them to the lab. Everyone will work on their own computer. If your writing is finished you have three choices: see Mr. C. to conference about revision, work on another piece of writing, perhaps for our upcoming publication, or go to a desk to read. There are classes where I allow the students to conference on their writing in the lab. However, in one month I have had too many experiences where students end up WAY off task, goofing around, arguing, throwing things, and so forth, so conferencing is done between students in a highly structured setting in the classroom.

On the way to the lab, no fewer than seven students, nearly one-third of the class, plead desperately to go their lockers. This leaves me with two choices: one, if I allow them to go, it will encourage this behavior, and every time we go to the lab there will be a parade to the lockers; two, if I forbid them, I have effectively excused them from working for the period and they will proceed to disrupt the others. They go to the lockers. We enter the lab and Ed (of the Cult of Ten Thousand Questions) finds me. I sometimes wonder if Ed is able to get out of bed and to brush his teeth without stopping to ask his parents a few dozen questions. Ed wants to know (again) exactly how long the writing has to be. I explain (again) that there is not a length requirement. I am looking for quality, not quantity. He also wants to know how many times during the next week we will be going to the lab, if he should save his work on his own disk or one of mine, and if he can choose his own computer. I am saddened by Ed. He is a very nice person and an intelligent student. However, I doubt that he will ever be gainfully employed because the employer will not be able to ask HIM any questions, given Ed's steady barrage of inquisition. After Ed, I buzz around the room, helping students boot up and get going. I ask Jason to move away from Levi, Ryan to avoid Chad, and so on. After ten minutes most of the students are hard at work.

The students are working on the second part of their autobiography assignments. For both sections, the students have had a wide variety of choices for both writing and the visual component of the assignment. I went through a half dozen canned autobiography manuals and pulled and mutated and just plain made up some. Kids can basically write on anything related to their lives or those of their families, as long as they make a sincere effort to make it truthful. There have been pieces about family trips, holidays, deaths, births, illnesses. Students have written about school experiences, excursions with friends, hunting, fishing, and all sorts of Alaskan kinds of adventures with planes, boats, and snowmachines. The vast majority of these pieces are uplifting, happy memories. However, in this class in particular, there have been some brutal recollections of abuse. One of my most conscientious students wrote about how she and her sister were nearly starved, to the point of eating their own hair, before they were removed from their own birth parents. There was an account of a gang rape of three twelve-year-old girls by some high school students. I could go on. I guess I didn't anticipate this aspect of the autobiographies. I've asked students to write on a whole range of autobiographical writing over the years, but never to this extent. In talking with Peggy Turner, a colleague in Guntown, Mississippi, I found that she too was somewhat startled by some of the narratives that were unleashed. Several of us are asking our students to write autobiographies as a prelude to an upcoming literary exchange on *Anne Frank: The Diary of a Young Girl*. We also have been reading a great deal of nonfiction and autobiographical writing, and I think that has triggered some of these memories. I talked to the counselor about some of the things that have emerged, and she said that it was actually a good sign that the students were writing about such things. It is a sign that they are coping and attempting to leave it behind. I had considered doing a major piece of teacher research on the autobiography assignment. But, once we were involved in the autobiographies, I found that my time commitment was so intense, reading and responding to the kids' works in progress, that I could only manage a cursory journal entry from time to time. Perhaps next time, now that I have a better idea of how to sequence and pace the assignment for the students and me, I will be better equipped to conduct some research while it is happening.

I do want to include a couple of examples of writing that have emerged from the autobiography assignment and to comment on them. Some are light, some very dark. One of the suggested topics for students to write on was "My Future." I left this wide open, suggesting that they could write about a day in the future, their careers, their families, their living situations, whatever. Jamie, who is a very pleasant student with a positive attitude, wrote about her future.

> I hope in my future I will be rich. I plan to get this way because the richest man of earth will be my grandfather, and since he liked me I will inherit all of his money. I plan to live in a castle with fifteen floors. The first ten floors will be just for my animals. I plan to let the ocean flow into my castle during high tide for all of my sea life. (Although the water could never go up farther than the first three floors.) I will have every animal, except snakes, and the animals could come and go on the drawbridge.

In case you are wondering, none of the future pieces in any way mentioned working for a living, except for one piece about playing in the NBA, if that is considered work. What I did enjoy about pieces like this one were the vivid and incredible imaginations that emerged.

I have taught in my own version of Nancie Atwell's writing workshop, and have written about that experience. I agree with the principles behind it and found that it was a very effective model, with my own mutations for teaching writing. However, I chose not to have a formal writing workshop this year. Why not? Well, I only have the students for forty-five-minute periods, when before we were together for lovely one hundred-minute blocks. Also, at Bread Loaf, I talked with Michael Armstrong about revision and about providing quality aesthetic responses to students regarding their writing. In order to establish this literary community, we must have a common language and common texts as a means to discuss the students' work. It is important for students to select their own topics for their writing, but I don't see a problem with providing a framework for them to operate in. For instance, this first quarter we were working on nonfiction. I could be convinced to accept just about any work of nonfiction as part of the autobiography assignment; this allowed me to focus the readings and the mini-lessons to the task at hand as a framework. Certainly there are students who would rather be writing poetry, or plays, or fiction, but they will get that opportunity during the school year. (In fact, they can do it right now, conference with me, and submit it to our mini-literary magazine on their own, as a few students have done.) Two other important considerations led to this framework. There are students, particularly at the beginning of the school year, who want and need a framework to get going. Secondly, as William Kittredge used to say, "You have to write about your own backyard, and do it well, before you can take your readers with you to Mars." In other words, start with what you know. It could be said that autobiographies force students to take unnecessary risks in their writing, by forcing them to present themselves (a sacred notion) on paper, and that it would actually be less intimidating to write about "Mars" to begin with. Well, I've taken several steps to keep this low-risk. There are several no-risk choices for students to select. Topics such as "A Day In the Life," or reminiscences about times when they were successful, or places they have been do not require heartfelt sharing of personal information. As a whole, I think the project worked well. This piece of writing is also an example of the old "teacher as writer" maxim. If I'm going to ask my kids to write a "Day in the Life" piece, I should be writing one also.

We are talking about the area where theory meets practice. In order to reconcile our beliefs with what we are actually doing in the classroom there is a chain of decisions. Sometimes this chain leads down the wrong path and one of two things happens: we are absolutely convinced that we are doing the right thing philosophically in the classroom, but the practice bombs with the kids; or, even though we feel as though we have compromised our beliefs, the practice works, or seems to. My point here is that for the first time in my teaching experience I feel as though there is a positive, productive meshing of the theory and the practice. I still need to make adjustments. For instance, this population still views revision as "copying over." So we need to do a lot of training there. The students are more dependent on me for direction than I would like, but all in all the program is producing quality writing and a good healthy exchange of ideas, both in writing and orally, about our readings. Before we return to the next autobiography sample, and to my second-hour class, let me say that it is this sense of purposeful direction in my practice that has resulted in a very positive attitude, a feeling of satisfaction. I'll talk more about this later, but it feels good to see genuine creativity in the classroom. So often the writing reflects little investment or is void of the lively voices that I hear all day. Pat D'Arcy, who wrote *Making Sense, Shaping Meaning*, suggested that we have to focus on the *drawing out* of our students and not the pouring in. We have to realize that we have living, breathing, thinking human beings in the classroom who bring with them an immense package of experience, emotion, insight, and reflection *to* the classroom. So when I read about Jamie's castle, I think about other ways to spend my time and I genuinely feel that I am where I should be.

Back in the computer lab, the girls have now abandoned their writing. The computers are off, the chairs are huddled, and although the girls make feeble attempts to make it look as if they are doing something productive when I draw near, it is obvious that they are now in a purely social mode. Twice I ask them nicely to return to work. The third time, when I overhear gossip about who didn't call who what, I select places for them to work, on opposite sides of the room. Obviously, this won't inspire them to pick up their notebooks or to turn on the computers and to write great thoughts, but I need to reestablish our relationship. There is a substantial amount of freedom when it comes to written expression; however, when it is time to work, I mean business, especially when it comes to the rights of others. I never bought into the assertive discipline business. I saw it as a marketing device for fascism, but that doesn't mean that my classroom is a teen recreational center either. Two of the girls get very angry, stomp away, and pout for the rest of the period. Such is life. I continue to buzz around. I notice that someone has sent a few obscene messages to the printer. I happen to glance at Will and know instantly, as our eyes meet and are quickly diverted, that it is he who has sent them. Will loses his computer privileges for the day, maybe longer, and returns to a desk.

Will has been failing most of his classes since third grade. He is obviously bright, so he has never been retained. I'll spare you the details, but suffice it to say that he has had an extremely difficult home life for as long as he can remember. Even the basic principles of cleanliness are not present. I would like to write about all of the wonderful things that I am doing to "save" Will, to finally be the one adult who rescues him from his hopeless plight. It won't happen. When I first started teaching I used to lose sleep over kids like Will, and we all have them. I used to write long letters to parents and counselors and administrators. I used to try alternative reading materials and grading systems and positive notes and even small gifts. I don't do that anymore. Sure, I will treat him with respect, maybe give him an extra benefit of the doubt from time to time, maybe go out of my way to give him some positive encouragement whenever possible. But . . . I won't sacrifice the learning of others in order to work with Will. It is a cold, hard fact that my chances, during a forty-five-minute period, of turning around eight years of school failure, are minuscule. Marilyn Buckley, one of the founders of the Berkeley Writing Project, said at a meeting once that "Hey . . . life is a do-it-yourself ball game. If you don't come to play . . . don't come." All that I can do for Will is to provide a safe, caring environment for learning, construct a program which is interesting and allows for the wide diversity of ability and interest levels, and allow him to succeed on his own terms. If he makes it, it will be because he has chosen to. I can't make that decision for him. Out of ninety-three students in the eighth grade, eight have failed the first quarter. There was a time when I would have been alarmed by this. Now I realize that these kids have priorities that are different from mine. Unfortunately, I, and most of us, teach in a system where we only have one menu to choose from. We end up pounding square pegs into round holes until the pegs either break or change. And you know which usually happens. Suffice it to say that there is only so much time in a school day. Jamie, and Jessica, whose poem we will read shortly, need and deserve as much time with the coach as Will. After all, they've come to play.

I mentioned how highly I regard my first-hour class, the respect and admiration I have for my ninth graders. But, in my third-hour class we have a 220-volt connection. We're plugged in. A fluke in the scheduling has resulted in the enrollment of only eleven students during this period. Periods two, four, and five have about thirty each. Here, after my challenging group leaves, I find sanctuary. I write different lessons plans for them. I choose different reading selections for them. They are my conduit to the all powerful education life force.

Today, we are going out: I have the keys to the school van. The vice principal is covering my fourth-period class. We have all the provisions for a weenie roast on an open fire. It is not raining. The students are dressed warmly and are smiling, laughing. If it were up to me, we would all teach in little portable classrooms with garages behind them. Whenever we felt the calling, we'd put down the books, hop in the van and go to the ocean, the mountains, the forest, the rivers and lakes, the libraries, the colleges . . . you bet. That might not ever be a reality. However, mindful of the urging of my Bread Loaf colleague Bill Rich back in Vermont, the students and I decided as a group to do some nature writing. We read "The Dream" by Wendell Berry and discussed it for an entire period.

> I dream an inescapable dream
> in which I take away from the country
> the bridges and roads . . . (64)

This, then, begins the process of placing ourselves in the outdoors. The idea of our role in the natural world was a lively topic. We also read "Birches" by Robert Frost. At a meeting a few years ago, Marilyn Buckley walked in and recited this poem from memory, beautifully. It has since been a very important work to me. Reading the poem with the students led to a discussion about natural images as metaphor. We made a list of all of our supplies and signed up to go to Bishop Creek.

In the van the kids are laughing, singing along with the radio, whispering. You can feel their excitement. Bishop Creek is about ten miles down the road from the school. You turn off three miles from the end of the road which begins in Anchorage. On the way we see a few swans on still lakes, ducks making their escape over the trees. There are a few leaves remaining, but most are gone. As we leave the van, the forest has a surreal quality, misty, with a slight musty odor of decay. The air is heavy and warm. There are no cars in the parking lot.

We walk to the bluff, less than a mile from the van, and leave our supplies at a campsite over looking the inlet. Oddly, everyone is quiet for a moment. We stand looking out at the expanse of mud and open water, the mountains on the other side fading in and out of the fog. I breathe deeply with the recognition that it is so good, so invigorating to be away from the school. It is like that first moment when you dive into a lake on a hot day; for a moment your heart races, your other senses dulled by the rush of cool exhilaration. We walk along the beach for a few hundred yards. The kids split into pairs and threes; some walk alone. A few join me for a while. We look up to see two eagles, one large mature bird and one yearling, perched atop two bald cottonwoods. Their eyes follow us as we walk not ten yards from their observation posts. After a mile or so, I ask the kids to spread out and find a place to sit and write. I would have liked to have just spent the day, and then the students could write as the spirit moved them, but we do need to return for class after lunch. With the absence of bells, fluorescent lights, and the separateness of thinking that school so often requires, I hope there might be a moment when the "stillness" that Rilke writes of reaches us. Soon it is absolutely silent, except for a few distant planes, the water on the beach, the faint breeze in the trees, and the words come.

> Moist air,
> running stream,
> cloudy skies,
> Fall is coming,
> creeping, crawling
>
> Leafless trees
> slumping over
> steep hills.
> Eagles looking
> for their prey.
> Tide's out,
> way out.
> Fall is coming,
> rumbling, roaring

Little clams are
washed up on shore.
Moose tracks,
rusty-colored
grass, birds
chirping.
Fall is coming
it's coming,

It's here. . . .

　　Amy Hutchings

Amy's poem went through an interesting progression from prose to poetry. She is almost painfully shy; it was only after much prodding that she agreed to go public with the piece. It's always interesting to me to try to decide whether middle school students are genuinely reluctant to share their writing because they are insecure about it, or whether they are in fact manipulating the teacher into praising them profusely. With Amy, it is the former. She received response from the large group, a group of three students, and then (because of the small number of students in the class) from me, during an extended conference. Her poem reveals a sincere effort to express herself in a unique way, to convey her thoughts and emotions from that time.

Jessica's writing does the same. This is one of my all-time favorite student poems.

The Stirring

I look out across the sea,
mist blurring my vision,
I see to a certain distance,
then all is lost.
Yet, I see a glimpse of mountain peaks,
looming high, like my future.
The ocean,
still as the dark sand
calls me softly.
Rocks protrude from still water,
little islands,
refuge for stranded creatures.

I sit on the damp sand,
breathe moist air,
listening to far off planes.
My mother's face appears,
I remember all she tells about nature.
"If I die, I want to be buried in the outdoors."
We used to walk along the beach,
side by side, talking,
sometimes silent.

I see fallen trees,
whose roots branch out with twisting arms,
as if to take me to the unknown.

Two eagles,
like my mother and I,
always close,
but still drifting.

　　　Jessica Moore

"A glimpse of mountain peaks, looming high, like my future." Here is the jus-
tification for relevant learning activities for kids, for abandoning endless skill-
and-drill routines, for asking students to look within instead of merely
pouring in content. Jessica's poem is a powerful statement that young people
have rich and colorful ideas that need an outlet. It is my job to set the stage
where this can happen. In looking back at this poem at the end of the school
year, I realized that it was one of the highlights, a reason for celebrating. Too
often kids force their ideas in poetry into rhyme, often losing the meaning. Or
they attempt to be so profound and to grasp such huge abstractions that the
poetry either makes no sense, or is trite and cliché ridden. Jessica has displayed the rare ability, or perhaps the gift, to speak from the heart.

　　When we return from the walk and the writing, we build a fire and roast
hot dogs and marshmallows. Then we read our pieces around the circle. It is
fascinating to see how differently each student records the experience of sitting
on the beach. As I listen to them read, it dawns on me again how rarely we ask
students to make connections between ideas, activities, experiences, and their
own lives. After a round of spontaneous applause, we have some time left so
they scamper down to the stream. Soon they are tossing out logs and bombard-
ing them with rocks, hooting and hollering, sliding in the mud, having serious
fun—another reminder that eighth graders, in their natural state, resemble elementary students more than high school students, although I'm not certain the
senior high students wouldn't be engaged in the same wanton horseplay.

　　Bishop Creek has been a spiritual place for me during the last two
years. There are many beautiful areas on the Kenai River, on the Inlet, on the
many lakes and streams, but for some reason this place has a palpable sooth-
ing quality in the air. Despite the parking lot, there are usually few people
there, with the exception of walkers on the beach. Almost exactly one year
ago, I took my children—Paul, age two, and Hannah, age five—to this spot.
While they were playing near the water, I had time to write a poem.

Bishop Creek, Labor Day

Smoky clouds edge
the heavy blue sky,
and jagged white peaks.

The sun is trapped
in twisting ribbons
of pure white light,
streaking through the hard brown mud,
still wet from the ebbing tide.

The inlet beyond, rocking gently
whooshing, wavering blue-gray,
blue-white.

This morning is so crisp, tight,
almost cold, that it seems with
each breath, the mountains draw near,

———

Paul packs the smooth wet rocks
into bulging cheeks and gurgles happily
"Nikgh! Nikgh?"

Hannah places sticks, black moss
rocks, pieces of shell
into a mound of wet sand
"and the house has windows
and plates and forks. . . ."

———

An eagle drops,
skims the creek and veers upward
with talons empty.

One yellow cottonwood,
sliding first into fall— a candlelight
flickering in the breeze—
against the sullen spruce.

To the north
immense gray boulders
lean haphazardly, as if thrown
like pebbles from the moon.

Sitting on a bleached white log
watching my children in this world . . .

My heart is full.

I look back at this poem now as more of a letter to myself, a written example of the novelization of our lives, than a literary work. I was reminding myself to cherish my children and the natural beauty of this place. With the students on the field trip, it dawned on me in a startling way that all of them are someone's children. That sounds like a naive notion. But one of the most powerful impacts of parenting on my teaching has been this very idea. I now look at students more as the greatest hopes of their parents and as individuals who began as helpless infants carried in their parents' arms. I think teachers have a tendency to transfer adult expectations to the students. Having your own children, helping them to tie their shoes, listening to them learn to read, hearing their questions about the planets and animals and all of the mysteries of the world brings those expectations back to reality. I keep reminding myself that it was only a few short years ago that my eighth graders were learning to write cursive, to read entire books on their own, to play outside without supervision. Of course, I transfer my own beliefs as a parent to the imagined parents waiting at home for my students. This is also an unrealistic pitfall. The autobiographies were a stark reminder that there are parents who are unable to provide a basic level of sustenance to their children, let alone to spend a day on the beach with them.

———————

Sometimes, in looking back at even a short slice of life from the classroom like "A Day in the Life," I wonder how it is that we survive in such a complicated, demanding, and constantly evolving environment, *and* make sense of any of it. One of the things that I wrote about in my original journal version was the need for quiet, for stillness, and for reflection. I go to work very early every morning to prepare for the day, to respond to student writing, to take care of the many things that must be done. But I also find time in the morning to listen to music, to drink coffee, to write about what is happening, and to sit and think. When I first began reading teacher research and meeting other teacher researchers, I was simply blown away by the universe of possibilities to think about, to write about. When I first began writing about the classroom, it felt good to get some words down, to begin to sort out the deluge of intuitions, observations, and speculations rushing by. For three years I worked closely with a good friend, and we would exchange e-mail almost daily. Since we shared students, athletes, and administrators and worked on the same collaborative team, the common context provided a great framework for discussing these issues. Those notes, journal entries, letters, and focused reflections (like the "A Day in the Life" piece) not only provide artifacts for future study, but force us to be more systematic in our role as *learners*, and not merely facilitators and managers influenced by the many forces *outside* our classroom. There are many, many voices in the chorus singing about what should happen in the classroom, from district-level administrators, to school board members, to ten-pound curriculum guides. And, sadly, the most important, knowledgeable, and relevant voices are often absent. The voices of our students need to guide our practice. Thankfully, the student voices in the Anne Frank Conference are colorful and powerful enough to demand our attention and careful examination.

2 The Anne Frank Conference

Beginning in the summer of 1992, teachers from rural schools in six states—Arizona, Alaska, Vermont, South Carolina, Mississippi, and New Mexico—were invited to study at the Bread Loaf School of English near Middlebury, Vermont. Funded by fellowships from the DeWitt Wallace/Reader's Digest Fund these teachers were to create from their work together the Bread Loaf Rural Teacher Network (BLRTN). The concept of creating such a network grew from the recognition that rural teachers have limited staff development and collaboration opportunities, as compared to teachers in urban areas, and that rural schools generally lag behind the mainstream in education in terms of technology and (often) equity of funding. The resulting Bread Loaf Rural Teachers Network would subsequently provide a desperately needed support system for rural teachers.

The main communication tool for the BLRTN would be the telecommunications network known as BreadNet that was already in place for students and alumni of the Bread Loaf School of English. Over the summer of 1992, the selected teachers met to plan projects that would take advantage of telecommunications for connecting their students in collaborative work. The first such project that would result from their efforts would be the Anne Frank Conference, to be discussed in detail later in this chapter.

It is important to know that the Anne Frank Conference and the projects that BLRTN teachers and students engage in are not "technology projects." They are quality, collaborative studies and inquiries that use telecommunications as a tool. When the projects are most effective, the technology becomes nearly invisible. There is some basic computer literacy necessary to participate in these kinds of activities, but it is minimal. Most teachers with even a passive working knowledge of word processing can acquire the needed expertise to communicate online in a very short amount of time. In addition to the intensive study of literature and writing over the summer, the teachers at Bread Loaf also learned to use FirstClass, a software application for telecommunications. This application is a user-friendly program. It operates entirely by pull-down menus, from which one selects the commands to use, and icons (small pictures) that symbolize the different areas within BreadNet. Using this simple program, we, the BLRTN participants, practiced sending notes to one another over the summer and made plans for our classrooms in the fall.

That online communication reflected and extended the thought-provoking discussions we had begun in person at Bread Loaf. As English teachers, we attempt to make sense of our world through our peers, just as adolescents do, though we are perhaps more reluctant and self-concious as a group than our students are. In the summer of 1992, the dinner tables at the inn of Bread Loaf School of English had provided an ideal forum for frank discussions with peers about literacy, literature, school, and life. It was in that setting that Peggy Turner and Mary Burnham first began to discuss the idea of creating an electronic classroom for students reading *Anne Frank: The Diary of a Young Girl*.

After that initial discussion, the idea was batted around in various ways until someone eventually mentioned it on BreadNet. The idea of creating an online student literary conference using BreadNet generated enthusiastic response. Peggy Turner, from Guntown, Mississippi; Sondra Porter, Talkeetna, Alaska; Mary Burnham, Newbury, Vermont; Dixie Goswami (Coordinator of BLRTN), Caroline Eisner (Technical Consultant to BLRTN), and I sent electronic messages back and forth about how, when, and what this conference might be. In an audio conference, Tom McKenna of Unalaska, Alaska, joined the group, and we decided to begin a cycle of written responses to *Anne Frank: The Diary of a Young Girl*. We selected this text for several reasons: it was a book we were all familiar with as teachers; it is a challenging text for eighth graders, but one that is accessible because of Anne's candid discussion of issues pertinent to adolescents; and it was a book that we all had copies of in our classrooms.

After another, extended audio conference in November of 1992, we determined the specifics of the online project. To begin the online discussion of the Anne Frank diary, we agreed that each class would post a "prompt," which could be a question, a comment regarding a particular passage, a series of opinions or reflections, or anything the "prompting" class chose to do. The other classes would then respond in writing, online, to the prompt. We decided to begin just after Christmas, following two weeks of prereading activities relating to WWII and the Holocaust. The online literary exchange would be called the Anne Frank Conference. We were ready to roll.

The first Anne Frank Conference, in which students and teachers exchanged writing through BreadNet, lasted for about seven weeks. After that first conference concluded in 1993, Caroline Eisner created a transcript of the entire exchange, which became the basis for the initial study of the writing that transpired. This book is based on the first three years of the conference; representative exchanges from those three years will be discussed in subsequent chapters.

Returning to the organization of that first Anne Frank Conference, I would like to present the basics for setting up the online exchange and describe how the project looked in each participating classroom. When a teacher logs onto BreadNet, using FirstClass, the first screen that appears has several options, including a personal mailbox for correspondence. The first screen looks like this:

Within the folder labeled "Conferences" there are folders that contain conferences on topics ranging from Alternative Assessment, Chaucer, To Kill a Mockingbird, and Teacher Research to Nature Writing and

Shakespeare. When the "Anne Frank Conference" folder is opened, this
is what appears on the screen:

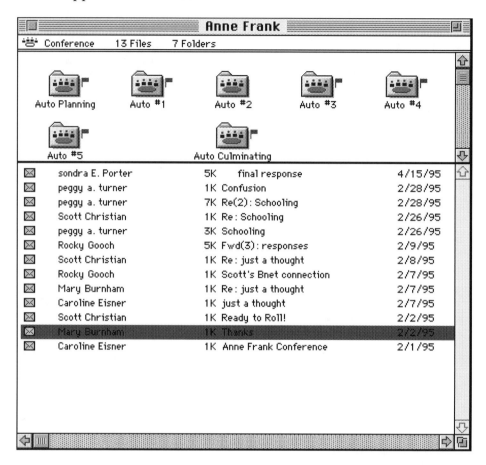

Each little picture, or icon, at the top of the screen represents a folder, in
which communication among the different classes is organized. "Auto
Planning" refers to Autobiography Planning. In this folder, the teachers discussed prereading strategies, the timeline for the conference,
outside reading materials, films, and so on. The folders labeled "Auto
#1-#5" were created so that the discussion for each week of the confer-
ence would begin in one location. With more than three hundred students potentially participating in the conference, this system would
allow us to quickly see the responses for each week without scrolling
through numerous messages as the conference progressed. You can
think of each of these icons as representing a folder, or box, where each
student's writing was placed electronically. The final folder, "Auto

Culminating," was for the final writing and activities for the conferences. If you were to open the folder labeled "Auto #2" for the second week, you would see the following list:

⊠	sondra E. Porter	5K	response week 2 svhs	2/23/95	2:54 PM
⊠	Scott Christian	2K	Nikiski Again	2/19/95	7:38 PM
⊠	peggy a. turner	4K	Anne	2/19/95	4:02 PM
⊠	Mary Burnham	7K	New responses to Nikiski from	2/17/95	11:43 AM
⊠	Mary Burnham	1K	To helen	2/16/95	9:20 AM
⊠	Helena Fagan	3K	response from Juneau	2/16/95	1:17 AM
⊠	Mary Burnham	1K	Re: Nik. Prompt 2	2/15/95	10:54 AM
⊠	Scott Christian	1K	Nik. Prompt 2	2/15/95	12:02 AM
⊠	Mary Burnham	1K	Response	2/14/95	1:25 PM
⊠	Scott Christian	1K	Nikiski Prompt	2/13/95	10:36 PM

Auto #2 — Conference   10 Files   0 Folders

The messages are listed with the most recent at the top of the list. At the bottom of the list is a message titled "Nikiski Prompt." Each week a predetermined class would post a question or prompt for the other four classes to respond to. During the second week it was our turn. Then, the other classes would respond to our prompt, placing their responses in the "Auto #2" folder, so they wouldn't be confused with the writing from the first week. This "Auto #2" screen is an actual list from week two of the second year of the Anne Frank Conference, which featured the same structure as the original conference, but included a new teacher, Helena Fagan from Juneau, Alaska, and her students.

This working format might not be entirely clear yet, but as we look at the five classrooms in the original conference, the basic system should become more understandable. I'd like to emphasize that *none* of the teachers in the original conference were computer or technology instructors. All of us were English teachers with widely varying experience with computers. Before that first summer at Bread Loaf, Tom McKenna had been the only teacher with extensive telecommunications experience. The rest of us were novices.

Before we look at the actual exchange of student writing, and what happened there, I think it is critical that we put this conference into the context of the five classrooms. The writing that took place within the online conference was only a small aspect of a rich and complex learning sequence in the different classrooms. These sequences varied greatly from one classroom to the next, with the unifying factors being the reading and thoughtful analysis of text through various forms of written response, discussion, improvisation, and visual art. None of the classrooms involved in this project were "gifted and talented" classes. My purpose here is not to draw conclusions about these different settings, but to firmly establish the idea that collaboration on a project such as this does not mean the loss of independence in terms of a teacher's pedagogy or style. Instead, it is a drawing out of the strengths and creative ideas and visions that enhance all of the classrooms and make for a more compelling experience for all of the students. I also want to suggest that it was truly *the students* who turned this conference into a relevant, meaningful exchange. The teachers merely set the stage and became facilitators as the students made this project their own. The next section gives a brief sketch of each class that participated, based on the online and telephone discussions that took place during the conference, together with some follow-up reflections in response to my questions regarding the context of the project.

I'd like to emphasize that these sketches of the teachers who participated, the communities and schools where we teach, and the types of activity and learning processes that were occurring in the classrooms are intended merely to provide a general feel for the learning environments within the conference. A book could be written on any one of the classrooms if there were a deliberate attempt to catalog the activities and explain the theory and infinite variables that surround them. Sondra Porter, Peggy Turner, Tom McKenna, Mary Burnham, and I participated in the first year of the conference; Helena Fagan's classroom joined during the second year; and Phil Sittnick's students participated in the third year.

Sondra Porter, Talkeetna, Alaska

Sondra Porter is the consummate rural teacher. She has lived and taught in Trapper Creek, Alaska, near Denali National Park (home of Mount McKinley, also known as Denali) in central Alaska for twenty years. The central industry in the area is tourism. Her school, Susitna Valley (known as Su-Valley) Junior/Senior High School was built in 1973, the year she arrived. There are approximately 190 students in grades 7-12. Sondra is the only full-time English teacher at the school, where she teaches literature, composition, speech, and drama, and also performs many other duties and assignments as they arise. This school is located in one of the most scenic areas of Alaska, and, perhaps, the world. Sondra's students participate in a variety of outdoor activities including: hunting, fishing, skiing, hiking, camping, and riding snowmachines and four-wheelers. After twenty years in the classroom, many teachers experience burnout. Sondra, however, has been an energetic member of BLRTN and many professional organizations around the state.

Sondra Porter had one class of twenty-five eighth-grade students who participated. In the first year of the conference, the students wrote daily in journals. Next, they would work individually, in pairs, or in small groups to draft responses on three-by-five-inch index cards. Four students were then selected to take these to the computer lab where they were typed and saved on disk. Later, Sondra would upload the responses and send them to BreadNet. In addition to the writing, the students created a wonderful video introducing themselves and their school which featured several of their activities from the conference. The students wrote, performed, directed, and edited the video. My students were thrilled to see the people they had been writing to "live" on the video. Because of the enthusiasm of this connection, Sondra and I are talking about ways to get our students together in person as a culminating activity for the conference. Sondra's students also did role-playing activities and regular journal writing; during the second year, they wrote some interesting "chant poetry."

Mary Burnham, East Corinth, Vermont

Mary Burnham has taught at Waits River Valley School (WRVS) for thirteen years, nine years as a reading specialist, grades K-8, and the last four years as the middle school English teacher. The school has grown to 350 students and has gone through many changes over the years. For example, ten years ago the school burned down and the teachers and community pitched in to sort out the rubble and rebuild the school. Mary takes great pride in her school, noting that its teachers, because of budget constraints, are known as "the biggest scroungers in the region for recycling discarded furniture, books, and equipment from other schools." Since WRVS is truly a rural school, the students come from several communities and represent diverse socio-economic groups. The local towns seem to be the idyllic, pastoral Vermont settings of an earlier era. Each village has a general store, a post office, and a church. Although there are still many active dairy farms in the area, the number is steadily declining. Mary takes great pride in her school and her students, which is reflected in her work.

Mary worked with two separate eighth-grade classes on the Anne Frank Conference. The classes were heterogenously grouped with about twenty-four students in each class. For the duration of the conference, the students worked on some aspect of the study every day. They read entries from the diary, as well as the dramatized version. Mary says, "The kids wrote in journals or on BreadNet every day. They demanded it. Often I would have them write in their journals before writing on the disk to collect their thoughts." In Mary's classroom there was one Macintosh computer in the back of the room. Students would write their responses to the prompts on this one computer where they were saved on a floppy disk. Then, Mary would save the responses and send them to the other classes via BreadNet. Mary Burnham is the teacher who first mentioned the idea of "authentic audience" in terms of the students' writing. Perhaps her revelation was the result of observing what was happening in her classroom, where that one computer became the vehicle of transmission for hundreds of responses by her students. Mary discovered the beautiful and haunting book *Anne Frank: Beyond the Diary*, a photographic essay about Anne Frank and her family. Her recommendation of this book generated the creation of an online bibliography of supplemental texts used throughout the project. Mary's students studied anti-Semitism both in a historical context and its current manifestations; they also compared Anne Frank's actual diaries to the dramatization of the text. I think the best way to put this project into the context of Mary's classroom is to demonstrate the level of involvement by her students through one of her final comments on the exchange.

> A few minutes ago, on this gloomy Wednesday as we wait for another ice storm, my 8th graders on the Students Council came to me for an address. I wanted to share this unexpected measure of the success of our project with you all. I have used some materials from The Southern Poverty Law Center in Montgomery, Alabama, with my kids. They had just sent me materials on the white supremacist "Church" of the Creator, which is spreading the most vicious and violent material about Jews and Blacks I have seen this side of Hitler. After examining and talking about this in class, my kids, on their own and without talking to me, went to the Students Council and got them to donate $25.00 to the above center. I am so moved by this. Although I have felt that most of the kids were able to "walk" in Anne's shoes for a bit, this is better than any end-of-book test for showing that they really did "get it" about the Holocaust and the struggle for human rights that is still going on. I feel that, somehow, you all contributed to this success here in this most rural of Vermont towns. . . .

In Mary's room, the students determined their presence in the exchange; their writing was not filtered by, nor directed to, the teacher. Because they worked on the project in an environment of collaboration and independence, the students took charge of their study, eventually becoming social activists by taking their learning into the "real world" and having an impact.

Peggy Turner, Tupelo, Mississippi

Peggy Turner lives in Tupelo, Mississippi. She has been teaching English in Northern Mississippi for twenty-one years. She is currently teaching in Guntown, population 690, which is located in the northeastern corner of Mississippi. Peggy's teaching assignments vary from year to year, but two facts remain constant. First, she is highly respected by her peers, the local school administration, and the students in her classroom. Second, she sees between 140 and 165 students every day. Despite this incredible workload, and the responsibility that comes with it, she is continually exploring new methods of teaching and learning. At Guntown Middle School there are 450 students in grades 6 through 8. In describing her community, Peggy writes, "Guntown is a quiet community with strong rural traditions and values, which are constantly tested by forces of progress and change."

In Peggy Turner's classroom there was a wide array of activities happening throughout the second half of the school year. There were creative writing assignments, in which students speculated on the implications of a different outcome for the text, "rules for a happy life," imagined conversations between characters, and original scripts featuring ideas and characters from the book. The students also read and wrote book reviews on books they selected that were related to the Holocaust and its historical period. The students prepared interview questions for World War II veterans who visited the classroom. There were presentations featuring audiotape and videotape. Peggy recalls that the "room was full of their work," including models of the annex, maps, and artwork. I remember receiving an envelope during the exchange which featured a photo of two of Peggy's students wearing World War II uniforms. For the exchange, the students wrote individually and in small groups, usually after a general classroom discussion. Peggy would then spend long hours keying in the responses and sending them by modem to the other classes. In her room, like mine, the technology was invisible. The students did not have the opportunity to sit down and actually transmit their writing. One unique aspect of the conference format in Guntown was the establishment of a "teaching committee," a group of students who read the book beforehand and then helped to plan the activities in the classroom. Peggy, more than any other of the teachers in the conference, also wrote directly to the students within the conference as well. Considering that Peggy had 140 students, the logistics of this exchange, coupled with the momentum that developed, became a challenging but wonderful ordeal for her. One of the highlights of this whole experience for me was meeting Peggy at a BLRTN meeting in Taos the spring after the conference and seeing the Anne Frank notebook that she and her students had put together. This huge assemblage featured photographs of the activities in her classroom, artwork, poetry, and journal entries by her students, as well as excerpts from the online exchange. It was an impressive and rich document of the conference, an artifact demonstrating a depth of study in each classroom that went well beyond the online discussions.

Tom McKenna, Unalaska, Alaska

Moving farther northward, across the continent: of the Alaskan participants in the conference, Tom McKenna, from Unalaska, was from the southernmost point. Unalaska is a paradoxical place. Located nine hundred miles southwest of Anchorage (the nearest city), it is in many ways remote and rural despite its location in the heart of two of the nation's most lucrative and heavily industrialized fisheries, the Bering Sea bottomfish and crab fisheries. The character and composition of the student body in the Unalaska School District, a one-site, one-building district, is directly influenced by these geographic and economic contrasts. The most notable aspect of the student body is that it is in transition. Aleut youngsters still comprise a majority of the students who have moved from elementary grades through graduation; yet of the school's current population (about 320 students, K-12) only about 20 percent are indigenous to the island. A typical secondary class consists of ten or twelve students, about half of whom may have some Aleut ancestry. Other students most typically are from working families and have come from the Pacific Northwest as well as Vietnam, Japan, the Philippines, or other Pacific Rim countries.

In terms of the project, Tom McKenna's classroom was unique. His students were ninth graders; most other students in the conference were eighth graders. In what I think is a terrific model for literature study, Tom divided his class into groups and allowed his students to choose a text and an exchange. The Anne Frank diary students were working independently while other students in the same class were reading another text and participating in a different exchange. Tom acted as the monitor and advisor for the project, and one student acted as the "project manager." Describing the process, Tom wrote:

> Each day, I would set up some activity for the whole group, and then I would meet with the Anne Frank group just to touch base, to raise a few questions, etc. I tracked their participation in terms of holding them accountable for responses that they had agreed to write, but I did not usually participate in the development of their pieces, other than doing a final check on editing. Students in this small group rarely wrote or edited something that did not involve collaboration. Just because of classroom management concerns, I often would leave the students unattended, and then I would discover them comparing responses that they had written or urging someone to please finish their writing. . . . So, although one student was the editor in chief, the students were constantly asking others to help with spelling, punctuation, and editing.

The idea of dividing the class, allowing students to choose the text and exchanges to be involved in, is somewhat daunting, but exciting. Obviously, Tom had enough structure in place for the students to be successful, but also to be in charge of their learning. I think the setting in Tom's room significantly impacted the students' writing. I'll discuss this aspect later when we look at the exchange itself.

Helena Fagan, Juneau, Alaska

Juneau is the capital city of Alaska. Considered by some to be the most beautiful capital city in the United States, Juneau is located in a rain forest, with a stunning view of the surrounding mountains, overlooking Gastineau Channel. Originally fishing grounds for local Tlingit Indians, Juneau became a focus of attention in the late 1800s when Chief Kowee of the Auk Tlingit Tribe provided gold ore samples in response to a reward offered by a Sitka engineer. Soon, Juneau became a thriving mining town, grubstaked by Richard Harris and Joseph Juneau in August 1880. Although the mining industry has been through a typical cyclic pattern of near nonexistence, followed by occasional resurgences, the state government and the tourism, logging, and fishing industries have provided a stable base for the Juneau economy. Periodically there have been efforts to relocate the state government to a more central location, but (thankfully for the residents of Juneau) none of these efforts have been successful.

Dzantik'i Heeni Middle School was in its first year of existence when Helena Fagan, a teacher for seven years, and her students joined the Anne Frank Conference. In keeping with a middle school philosophy, Helena's students had selected the Holocaust as a project for their core, two-hour block of academic instruction. Reading the diary and responding to other students who were reading the book were only some aspects of a much larger study. In Helena's classroom were approximately thirty sixth-, seventh-, and eighth-grade students in a heterogeneous grouping of ability levels. Helena found that this project blended well with other classroom activities surrounding the Holocaust project. In addition to writing, students were involved in a variety of activities, including the reading of supplemental texts, interdisciplinary activities in social studies and science, viewing films, and small- and large-group discussions. Although all of Helena's students participated in the conference, not all of their writing was sent to the other classrooms in the exchange.

Helena is currently at work on her first book, very tentatively titled "Writing the Shadows: Life as a Daughter of a Holocaust Survivor." Throughout the exchange, I was impressed by the focused, thoughtful work that came from Helena's classroom. There is no doubt that her personal investment in the topic, as well as her ability to work within a multigraded, project-based structure, resulted in an opportunity where students could produce quality work.

Phillip Sittnick, Laguna, New Mexico

Phil Sittnick began teaching the same year that Laguna Middle School opened. This school, on the Laguna Pueblo Indian reservation in New Mexico, opened its doors as the first tribally designed, planned, built, and operated school in New Mexico. This school has received national attention for its innovative vision for the school in the community, and the truly collaborative nature of decision making. Based on the notion that the community is capable of running its own school and determining the educational future of its students, Laguna Middle School has found considerable success. The Laguna Pueblo reservation has about six thousand residents. It is located in west-central New Mexico, about fifty miles west of Albuquerque. This is high desert country at an elevation of six thousand feet. The pueblo has a relatively large reservation—two grocery stores, two gas stations, and one large employer, in addition to the tribe itself. Laguna Industries makes communications shelters for the United States military. There is also some ranching and some commuting to nearby towns for work.

Phil teaches the entire eighth-grade population at LMS in three classes, all of which participated in the Anne Frank conference, although not all students wrote online during the exchange. Teaching on a reservation, amid another culture, presents unique challenges to teachers from outside the reservation. Phil, an intelligent, articulate teacher, has been diligent about communicating with people in the community to determine what kinds of topics and techniques are appropriate in the classroom. Naturally, the students from Laguna had different perspectives on the reading of the diary, particularly about the relationships among the people in the Annex. Later in the book, we'll look at the diversity of views which were expressed, including a close analysis of an exchange in which Phil's class dominated the discussion.

Scott Christian, Nikiski, Alaska

Again moving to the north, we arrive in Nikiski, Alaska, a small town on the coast of Cook Inlet on Kenai Peninsula. Like Tom McKenna's Unalaska, Nikiski is also a paradoxical place. On one hand, there is the stunning beauty of Mount Redoubt across the Inlet, the image of beluga whales rolling through the mouth of the Kenai river, and the stunning beauty of the maze of rivers and streams that pass through a nearly pristine wilderness when you leave the highway. In contrast to that image, the one highway that leads to our community is lined with small petroleum-related businesses, a large fertilizer plant, and an oil refinery, reflecting the major source of income for the people in our region: the petroleum industry. The inlet is dotted with oil platforms and frequented by tankers. This same water is also the source of the peninsula's second major income: fisheries. As for the school, Nikiski Senior/Middle School was opened in 1988. It is a beautiful facility with approximately five hundred students in grades 7-12. Nineteen ninety-three was my first year at Nikiski and my ninth year of teaching.

I had four classes of approximately twenty-five students participating in the conference. As in the other classrooms, there was a wide variety of activities taking place that related to the theme of the conference. One continuous strand was the writing in response journals. The students wrote in these journals throughout the year and were required to write at least once each week on a topic somehow related to the text. Often the students would open their journals and look through them before they wrote responses for the online exchange. My major concern, which I managed well at times, and not so well at other times, was the sheer volume of responses and writing. We posted our responses in different ways. Sometimes the students would write individually on three-by-five-inch index cards and then I would have a group of students select which responses to send. Once, I sent all of the responses from one class. Another time, the students wrote in groups of threes and fours; sometimes they wrote in pairs. Usually, I would ask my student aide to key the responses into the computer, and then I would take the disk home and post the responses in the conference. Often, I would end up doing a large portion of the keying in because of the quantity of responses. The volume both received and transmitted was a problem for all of us. The students also had an open-ended but formal writing exercise as the culminating event: they could choose from student responses and quotes from the book as a basis for a short essay. We also built a huge display in the library, researched the Holocaust, acted out short scenes, and improvised various ideas from the text in short skits.

———————

Clearly, there was a wide diversity of teaching experience, schools, and communities involved in the Anne Frank Conference. This diversity became a critical impetus for the wide range of opinions and experiences that were shared in the exchange. In reading these sketches again, I'm reminded of the factors that I think contributed to the success of this collaboration: the wealth of experience, the common philosophy, the willingness to take risks, and the desire to do something different in our classrooms in the quest for better learning. Most of all, I think there was from the beginning a very high level of trust among us, with each of us enjoying the opportunity to work with one another in the group. Aside from the professional issues of experience, commitment, and so on, I think the best test for selecting teachers with whom to collaborate is a simple question. Ask yourself if this person is someone whose company you'd enjoy over dinner or at a movie, or while riding across the state to a conference; if you can answer "yes" without reservation, chances are it will be a good collaboration. Cooperative work is not easy, and the current rhetoric about team teaching and interdisciplinary teaching doesn't always take into consideration the personal dimension of collaboration. You generally have to like the people you work with in order to create a good, new, complicated thing.

Now that you have a feel for what was happening in the classrooms, I would like to turn to the exchange of writing that took place online. Although the format was completely open in terms of what kinds of prompts we would post, or how many, a pattern emerged immediately that became the standard: taking turns, each group would post three questions as prompts. Why three? When we prepared to post our prompts, I had each class brainstorm as many ideas as possible; then we talked about them and eliminated some. The three questions that we posted were the ones that my students most wanted to write about. In talking with the other teachers, I found that it was common for the prompts to emerge largely from a group decision-making process. To roughly categorize the prompts, I'll use a model that I learned in college. These categories could be used to look at questioning strategies or responses, levels of discourse.

1. Emotional: Evokes happy, sad, angry emotions; a gut response.

2. Structural: Speaks of the text in literary terms: plot, character, climax.

3. Interpretive: Draws inferences on character motivation, discusses themes, patterns, symbolism, metaphor, goes beyond the literal.

4. Evaluative: Asks if the text "works" and why or why not. Looks at style and the effect of literary devices.

5. Generative (as opposed to reactive): Asks questions that are designed to elicit a personal response from the student that is based on the text, but moves into the student's real or imagined experience.

When we brainstormed our ideas in class the first prompt was clearly an emotional response question: "How would you feel if you went into hiding for a long time?" All the other questions were either strictly interpretive, such as "Do you think that Anne is conceited, arrogant? Support your answer." (there were two of these) or they were purely generative, not necessarily requiring interpretation, nor even a reading of the book. There were six of these, such as "We wondered if any of you can share family stories relating to World War II. Did any of your relatives serve in the war?" The last group of seven prompts combined levels four (evaluative) and two (structural), in questions such as "Which characters in the diary would you find it most difficult to live with if you were in the Annex? Explain why you would feel this way." Another example would be: "Why does Anne get along better with her father than her mother? Please relate this to your own experience." With each of these questions, the students are asked first to interpret the text, then to connect the ideas with their own life. What strikes me about these kinds of questions is that they are the kind that work best with middle school kids. When kids are trying so desperately to figure out who they are, questions that allow them to explore their own perceptions, opinions, and experiences are most effective. It's also part of the whole reader response movement, which suggests that this is a necessary part of the process of reading. The selection of the prompts was a mostly intuitive process by the groups of students. There was no discussion of "types of responses" or predictions about how students would react to the prompts; instead, it was a gut feeling that this type of question would be most effective.

I also think there is a strong likelihood that there were emotional, structural, interpretive, and evaluative responses that were happening in the classroom discussions and in the wide variety of other writings such as the response journals, book reviews, and essays that were not part of the exchange. This was the case in my classroom. We would often begin our discussions with level one questions and move around as the ideas progressed. Either I or a student would read an entry or two aloud. Then the students would have a quiet period to continue to read or to begin to write their thoughts in their response journals. Resuming discussion with the class, I would begin with literal questions about the entries, and try to lead students toward analyzing and interpreting the text, again through questions. It was only after these discussions, and often after reading prompts and responses from other classes, that the students wrote to the other classes in the conference. I can't generalize for all of the classes, but I have a sense that the online writing exchange was an extension of the literary dialogue which happened in the classroom. For my students, there was a tremendous amount of reading, discussing, prewriting, and writing that happened before their responses to the other classes. This is a critical notion in terms of the prompts, because I think the students were ready to connect the text to their lives.

The exception to this process would be the example of Tom's students, who, under the direction of the student "project manager," were largely working independently and did not participate in whole class discussions. However, these students were also a year older. As ninth graders, according to Tom, they occasionally were irritated with the "brevity and stereotypes" that were characteristic of some of the responses, particularly early in the exchange. In working with ninth-grade students, there often seems to be a strong yearning for independence, a desire to assert themselves as young adults, just entering high school. Perhaps these factors, and the fact that the students had been writing a great deal in other venues, facilitated the quality of responses that emerged from Unalaska.

Looking at the group of prompts as a whole, I see many points of entry—mostly "low-risk" kinds of questions—for kids to enter into the dialogue. Although these prompts allow and encourage some sophisticated kinds of responses, they are open-ended and do not imply an "answer." I have begun to speculate about what would happen in a text-based conference such as this, without prompts, in which the discussion between the students was truly open-ended. After looking at the relationship between the prompts and the writing that occurred, as well as at the development of the conversation, my hunch is that these prompts were critical in stimulating the dialogue. We'd have to try it out to actually see.

Perhaps the most important effect of the open-ended questions was that they allowed students the freedom to make their own connections between the text and their lives, and among themselves. Students were not constrained by narrow expectations in teachers' questions.

On the BLRTN audio conference that took place prior to the actual start of the Anne Frank Conference for students, we discussed what the prompts for writing would be like. At first we were referring to them as questions, but then we broadened the concept to include any kind of writing that would serve as a basis for the students to begin writing. In retrospect, it is interesting to note that we did not set any guidelines for these prompts, nor did we suggest what type of prompts might be most successful. The next section gives the prompts as they were posted in their sequential order.

Week One: Mary's Class

> 1. How would you feel if you had to go into hiding for a long time?
>
> 2. What would you do if you were living in Germany or Holland during the time we are studying?

Week Two: Peggy's Class

> 1. In order for us to learn more about your lives in Alaska and Vermont, we want you to pretend you have been in hiding for over two years, but now (in the present) rather than in the 1940s. After your liberation, you are given necessary medical attention and sent home. You are "badly in need of some rollicking fun," as Anne states on 12/24/43. How will you spend your first day home? Who will you see? What will you eat? Who will cook it? Where will you go? Be specific in naming and describing. We want some local color.
>
> 2. In Anne's room in the Secret Annex, the walls were decorated with pictures of movie stars, cutouts of babies, and a drawing of chimpanzees having a tea party. What would we find on your walls in your hiding place?
>
> 3. Try to explain more fully Anne's sense of frustration and disappointment as revealed in her 11/7/42 entry: "I only look at

her as a mother, and she just doesn't succeed in being that to me; I have to be my own mother." Consider and include what a mother should be by your standards, by society's standards; your inference, please, about what Anne is expecting, that she's not getting, and so on.

Week Three: Scott's Class

Part One:

1. Why does Anne get along better with her father than her mother? Please relate this to your own experience.

2. If you had to go into hiding in your area, where would you hide?

3. Do you think that Anne is conceited, arrogant? Support your answer.

Part Two:

As I was reading through the response log last week, I read an entry that brought up an interesting issue. Early on in the book, Anne discusses the "forwardness" of boys who blow kisses and try to hold your arm. This entry was in response to that section of the book. It was written by Theresa Petty and appears below as it was written as a free write in her response log. Feel free to respond as you see fit.

Mr. C.

Anne Frank is going through the same situation that our Jr. High goes through. Love and War might be what you call it. All of my girlfriends and I discuss who we like, and the agonizing questions of who might have a fancy for us. It's an ongoing cat-and-mouse game.

I always pondered on what people meant when they said "We're going out." I thought this meant a date. Actually, in Jr. High, this means you are officially boyfriend and girlfriend. Usually this relationship only lasts a week or two. In Jr. High the average is probably three days. Soon, a heart is broken because a person has another love. Then somebody gets the treatment of what is called being "dumped."

In the forties, boys treated girls differently than in the nineties. Then they carried books for you, and sweetly opened the door. I think boys act different today because the women made the movement of being equal. This gave the men a different perspective of how to treat the other gender. Even though this has occurred, boys and girls will go through lovesick crushes, and their hearts will beat like butterflies when the one they love walks by.

What do you think about the "movement of being equal"? Have things changed? If so, how? What does it mean to be "going out" in Mississippi and Vermont?

Theresa Petty, Nikiski, Alaska

Week Four: Sondra's Class

1. Which characters in the diary would you find it most difficult to live with if you were in the Annex? (Explain why you would feel this way.)

2. Some of us feel it might have been difficult for Peter and Anne to have a normal relationship. How would you act (feel) if you fell in love with someone you lived with who was not related to you?

3. We wondered if any of you can share family stories relating to World War II. Did any of your relatives serve in the war?

Week Five: Tom's Class

1. How do you think you would have put up with Mrs. Van Daan's bickering, complaining, and flirting? Would you have been as patient as Anne? Tell us what you would have said, done, and thought about Mrs. Van Daan. If not just Mrs. Van Daan, then anyone in the Annex.

2. What would you have written in your diary if you were staying with Anne and the others in the "Secret Annex"? Would your opinions have been the same about the people and situations around you?

3. Who was your favorite character in the book? Why did you enjoy this person's character so much?

Week Six (Culminating Activities): Mary's class

I know it is almost a cliché, but my kids started talking spontaneously about whether they agreed or not with Anne about "In spite of everything . . . I still believe people are good at heart." Then a girl brought in an old newspaper about Field Marshal Rommel and we started to talk about if he was as bad as Hitler, or was he "just a soldier?" (Mary's entry became the final prompt for many students in different classrooms.)

It is impossible to track which responses the students responded to the most, because only a portion of responses appeared online. Instead of looking at each prompt and the response to it, I think we can generalize that the more accessible the interpretive part of the question, and the more open-ended it was, the more successful it was. This isn't something new; it is probably something that all teachers have been doing for prompts for response journals, discussion, and formal writing assignments, but it is good to see this practice reaffirmed here. Not only was there terrific enthusiasm generated by the power of the students being connected across the country, there were also rich literary discussions, a variety of writing tasks, and a wide array of other types of interpretive and expressive activities happening that led to a great amount of quality writing. The prompts presented in this chapter also represent sound pedagogy, with students involved in the questioning process and asking generative questions. As you will see in the responses and the conversations that resulted from the prompts, this was an exchange of real substance, above and beyond the hype about surfing the Internet that we read about in the newspapers and magazines.

3 Performing, Reaching, and Connecting Writing

I think society today wants mothers to listen and obey a child's needs, but that isn't what being a mother is all about—just doing everything to please. It is about leading your child in a good, honest direction in life. Leading the way . . . giving the best advice. *I think Anne wants all the attention and her mother tries to keep her in the right direction, but Anne just doesn't follow.*

Kristen Hansen, Corinth, Vermont

I tend to agree with Anne Frank when I am happy with my life and in a good mood. Then I look at things and say, "Hey, things aren't really so bad . . . everybody is really good at heart." But when I get in a bad mood or I've just been in a fight, I think everyone is stupid and I wish they would grow up. Other times I just don't know what to think of people and I just can't understand them. This is sort of how I feel about Hitler. I just don't understand how he could kill so many people with a clear conscience without thinking twice. But did he think twice? Did he ever feel guilty? I guess we can never know.

Maria Heidenreich, Corinth, Vermont

For those of you who work with middle school students, and even for those of you who are *around* middle school students, I think you'll see something rare in the above writing. (Here, and throughout later student writing samples, the italics are mine.) These students are thoughtfully and seriously considering issues in a work of literature in the context of their own lives. I'm not saying that adolescents don't consider important issues in their lives and in literature seriously. In fact, they often are so preoccupied with issues like death and divorce and the pursuit of a happy life that they become depressed, as they haven't yet developed a framework in which to place these ideas. Furthermore kids frequently avoid this kind of thinking or writing because it is easier not to think about how people get along, or how parents should treat their children. It's much simpler to focus on the compelling and fascinating social world that is developing around them. Yet, once the conference was underway each year, this kind of thoughtful, purposeful writing was the norm, not the exception. When I started reading piece after piece of student writing, in which students were investing in the writing and offering what seemed to be sincere and considered views of pertinent issues, I was exhilarated.

In the previous chapter we looked at the nuts and bolts of the conference process. Now it is time to look closely at the writing. From the early days of planning the conference, through the final posting of our culminating writing, the teachers and students had a sense that we were involved in something unique and powerful. At the outset of the conference, we as teachers felt empowered by the recognition that we were truly the change agents at work on this project. There were no curriculum guides, no district-mandated scope and sequence, no state-mandated assessment that we were striving toward. We had a clean slate to create something relevant, meaningful, and academically challenging for our students. As rookies in the world of telecommunications, we were almost giddy with excitement over the ability to come home after work and talk to friends and colleagues around the country. In short, there was a tremendous amount of positive energy surrounding the start-up of the project.

I found myself looking with a more critical eye at what was coming through the wires, as well as at the writing my students were doing. Was all this extra effort—the added time to transfer the writing (which sometimes included keying in the pieces myself), not to mention the planning, online and through phone calls, and the audio conference—worth it? As soon as the first responses started coming in from the other classrooms, my students were thrilled. Throughout the six weeks of the conference it was not unusual to receive phone calls in the evening at home from students inquiring about incoming responses. They couldn't wait to read the writing and to respond. There were reluctant writers who were writing willingly without persuasion. But was the writing significantly different from the writing I had been reading for years in the response journals and in formal writing assignments and assessments? Occasionally a piece would come through that would really get my attention, through an analogy, a colorful voice, an image, a lively anecdote. I sensed intuitively that the writing was different, that it was better, more sincere, more lively than other writing I had seen in my classroom. But it wasn't until the next summer at Bread Loaf that I had the opportunity to look closely at the writing, to analyze it, and to make some tentative conclusions about its characteristics.

In order to put the taxonomy of writing categories and the ensuing discussion about the writing in context, I think it's important to provide a rough outline of the process that resulted in this completed work. (This narrative could be called The Quest for Understanding: A Teacher-Researcher with a Mission.) First, in the spring of 1994 I met with Dixie Goswami, a pioneer in the field of teacher research at the BLRTN meeting in Taos. There, I mentioned to her that there was something very different about the writing that had happened in the Anne Frank Conference. We talked about how excited the kids and teachers were and about the energy that consumed us during the project; I also showed Dixie a few samples of writing that were very different in voice, tone, flavor, and content than the writing I had previously seen in response to the diary. Earlier in my teaching, I had completed a couple of teacher research projects, and I knew that those persistent pangs of curiosity would yield fruit if I pursued them deliberately. I am a firm believer that, as teachers, we learn best from our students when we look closely at their learning and reflect purposely about these experiences in our own writing.

Next, Dixie asked Caroline Eisner, the technology coordinator for BLRTN, to create a transcript of the entire conference, which eventually totaled more than 120 pages. Then, at Bread Loaf in the summer of 1994, I took a course taught by Andrea Lunsford called Writing for Publication. After talking with Andrea, she and I decided that the first step toward understanding the writing was to read the transcript closely several times, looking for patterns, categories, anomalies, and so on. At first I was overwhelmed by the immense diversity of the content of the writing. The students had written about everything important in their lives. Regardless of the weekly prompts, important issues and topics organically came to the surface in their responses. While reading the transcript I categorized the responses according to their content, continually adding new categories and rereading until I was simply overwhelmed by the number of categories. Many responses had five or six different numbers next to them in the margin, indicating that they featured multiple-content topics. The box on page 48 shows the chart that resulted from this first look.

Although I could have continued categorizing the responses in this way for several more readings, I sensed that it wasn't the content alone that set this writing apart. Certainly it was remarkable that the students wrote about such a diversity of topics and issues. (The typical nonconference responses that happened in my classroom were much more focused on the questions at hand.) But of greater interest to me was the fact that as I was reading, certain responses, and exchanges would seem to leap off the page. I found myself putting stars and

Categories of Content

I. Emotional/Personal Needs/Growing Up	II. Text/Context of the book	III. Physical Needs/ Possessions/ Activities
Friends	History/Germany.	Pets
Siblings	War/Politics/ Government	Eating/Food
Parents/Divorce	Holocaust/Hitler/ Nazis	Toys (3/4-wheelers, skateboards, snowboards, snow machines, boats)
Family (including grandparents)	Prejudice	Sports
Home area/ Local culture	Survival	Hunting/Fishing/ Guns
Death/Suicide	Equal rights	Nature/Camping
Dating (boyfriends and girlfriends)	Anne's character	Popular culture (music, TV, movies, video games, comics)
Adolescence/ Growing up	Character of other people in the Annex	School
Hope, Despair, Loneliness, Anger	Emotional responses to the text	Telephone, Talking
Separating from friends, loved ones	Life in captivity	Grooming
Privacy	Responsibility/Blame	Sewing/Cooking
	Freedom	Shopping/Malls
	Evaluative comments on the book	Fashion/Style
		Reading
		Writing/Diaries
		Telecommunications

asterisks in different colors next to these responses, according my gut feeling that they were somehow different from the others. I then talked to Dixie, Andrea, and several teachers in the course taught by Andrea, explaining that I wasn't satisfied with my analysis of the content. I knew that there was something else about the writing that needed describing, but I couldn't explain how to describe it; I just knew they were there. Andrea suggested that I forget about describing the various kinds of writing. She proposed that I simply go with my largely intuitive sense of the different types of writing and categorize them accordingly, waiting to describe them until after I had separated them. This suggestion was very liberating. I spent two days in the library reading and rereading, using different symbols for what had now evolved into four different categories of writing. One category wasn't "better" or more "sophisticated" than the others; instead, the categories seemed to be different in terms of the purpose or the intent of the writing.

After putting the project aside for a couple of days to dwell on the work for my other classes, I returned and pulled out several responses that I felt belonged in separate categories. As soon as I began to do this I noticed two things. There were definitely unique traits present in each of the categories, although the lines between them weren't always clearly defined. I also discovered that I needed a fifth category to describe a special kind of writing; that was the first major Aha! of this project. At times throughout the conference, there were instances when students were using their writing online to communicate with one another in a completely different way. Although similar in some ways to spoken or telephone conversations, the responses also had characteristics of expository writing as well. It dawned on me that this type of writing needed a category all its own; I reached the final arrangement of five categories.

In reading the responses in the different categories, it was evident that there was an inordinately large frequency of thoughtful, sincere, sometimes experimental writing. There is good writing that happens in the eighth-grade language arts classroom. However, in nine years of teaching I had never seen so much quality, thoughtful writing occur with such frequency. There were responses to the prompts that seemed to leap off the page with an image of a writer who was striving to *connect* with her audience. I think this happened, among other reasons, because it was *allowed* to happen. As the prompts and responses arrived, the students had a great deal of liberty in terms of how they would respond. Also, the prompts were structured in a way that discouraged literal, short-answer responses, while allowing and encouraging the students to bring their own lives into the writing. After noting several of these examples of good, effective writing, I went back and examined several sections closely and reassured myself that the writing indeed seemed to fall into five basic categories, although at the time I had no idea how to describe them.

After another hiatus, during which I finished reading George Eliot's *Middlemarch*, wrote the graduate level form of a literary response (The Bread Loaf Paper), and ran a grueling 10K race in the hills of Vermont, I returned to the project to begin writing. After all, this was a Writing for Publication course, and all my multicolored symbols on the transcript and my lists and categories weren't going to be of much good unless I could turn it all into some sort of writing. I read and reread my categories. I printed a page with several responses from each category and hung it on the wall next to my desk in the library. I brainstormed a list of writing traits. I showed the writing to other teachers. I was stuck. I had no idea how to approach the description of these categories. It was one of those difficult times when, as a teacher, you not only question the specific matter at hand and consider alternative approaches, but you question the very foundations of your thinking. Is this project worthwhile? Will I learn anything from this? What does this have to do with the day-to-day job of teaching? Why don't I work in a bakery where I can take fresh rolls from the oven, breathe deeply, and know that they are good? There are so many layers, so many variables and considerations when we look closely at what happens in our classrooms, that at times it is like sitting in the middle of one of those spinning disks on the playground, the kind with bars that circle the outer edge, where you run alongside as fast you can, then jump on, lie down, and lean out upside down, gripping the bar tightly, and the world is a blur. That is the closest I can come to describing the mental muddle that I was in looking at this very complex and rich material.

Then, in a talk with Andrea, we had another major breakthrough. Andrea remarked that I could not in any way describe the writing in terms of what was happening in the mind of the writer during the writing. To generalize and suppose the mental processes of writers based on the writing samples was to walk on thin ice. The descriptions had to be focused on the writing samples themselves. After muddling around and getting nowhere, I boldly knocked on Dixie's door at about midnight, knowing that everyone is a night owl at Bread Loaf, and showed her my pages of responses and my lists of writing traits trying to describe them. It was then that she asked the central question that resulted in the taxonomy (described in detail later in this chapter) and my understanding about how this writing was different. Her simple, brilliant, twofold question resulted in the epiphany of the entire quest:

"What does the writing *do*? What is the *effect* on the reader?"

This, after all, is *the* central question that should be foremost in our minds when we as teachers sit down to read student writing. In reality, we find ourselves focused on any of the many and complex traits and considerations regarding writing when we read student work. Have students incorporated evidence from the text? Have they argued logically and clearly? Is the writing organized? Is there voice in the writing? Admittedly, I might also be asking, why is there still confusion about *to, too,* and *two* when we've looked at this problem from every possible angle for the previous two months? Responding to and understanding student writing is a complex task. But what writing does, and what its effect is on the reader should be the central question that drives our response and our writing programs.

Applying the question "What does the writing *do*? What is the *effect* on the reader?" to the student writing samples yielded five distinct answers.

1. The writing *performs* for the reader.
2. The writing *reaches* to an audience.
3. The writing *connects* with the reader.
4. The writing *strives to* connect with the reader in a unique and powerful way.
5. The writing *"talks"*; it incorporates elements of verbal conversation.

We did struggle for a while to find a term to describe what we called "striving writing," but otherwise these active verbs accurately described the effects of the student writing. I love the idea of writing as a tangible thing, a catalyst, a spark, a warm hand, a breath of cool air. Good writing is not lifeless; it is a living thing that sets forth with purpose and enters our lives. At times when I have read the responses to the class from the overhead transparency, or have listened as my students have drafted their responses, I have been genuinely lifted, buoyed by their energy, imagery, and thought-provoking analysis and discourse. After drafting and revising the taxonomy, I asked several teachers from the Writing for Publication class to evaluate sections of the transcript using the taxonomy. Although there wasn't a direct correspondence between their categorizations and mine, there was a high degree of similarity—enough so that I felt comfortable in moving forward, with some adjustments.

These descriptions are designed to describe the writing in terms of the effect the writing has on the reader. I also think they can be useful in our efforts to articulate to young writers just what it is that makes a piece of writing work. In order to encourage our students to be bold and to take risks with language, to connect with their readers, we have to understand the process that leads to that kind of writing. I'm not suggesting that there is a sequential order in this process, that students first write at level one, then move on to level two, and so on. I'm suggesting that there is a wide variety of types of writing that emerge when there isn't a clearly defined format or style described to the students beforehand. Different types of writing emerge at different times, depending on the students' interaction with the text, the implied reader or sense of audience, and—in this case—the prompt. These categories should be looked at as types of connectedness and forms of communicating, not as levels of proficiency. The following taxonomy is designed not to make assumptions about what was happening in the author's minds while they were writing, but to gauge their level of connectedness with the reader.

If you picture a Venn diagram, you'll understand that these categories have areas where they overlap. They are not clear steps in a linear process. A piece of writing might contain several common traits from one type and a few from another. There is some subjectivity involved in deciding where a piece of writing fits. The traits are *not* designed as a checklist, but as markers to indicate the type of writing.

Performing Writing: The writing seems disconnected from the reader

The first type of writing that appeared in the conference was largely "performing writing." The content of these kinds of written comments often consists of the kinds of statements that students make during the early phases of a class discussion. Since these statements have been taken out of the context of the student's writing process, it is difficult at times to interpret what the student is trying to say. The writing in this category is not very different from the kinds of writing we see every day in the classroom. The writer has a task at hand—to communicate an idea, to answer a question, to share an opinion—and the writer executes the task with what appears to be a low level of personal involvement.

The following first responses were in reply to a prompt from Mary's class during the first week: "How would you feel if you had to go into hiding for a long time? What would you do if you were living in Germany or Holland during the time we're studying?" I think they exemplify the concept of performing writing.

> If I went into hiding I would wish the war would get over soon.
>
> Brian Hartely, Talkeetna, Alaska

> I think the first thing I would do is to probably go visit my relatives, my friends and go shopping and go out and eat my favorite things.
>
> Chad Slaughter, Nikiski, Alaska

> If I were to go into hiding, I would put on my wall things that I liked, like snowboarding, and basketball, etc. But I would also

Taxonomy for Describing the Writing

Performing Writing: The writing seems disconnected from the reader.
- tends to be short, cursory comments
- is grounded in a literal reading of the text; concrete
- seems often to be knee-jerk response, without analysis or synthesis of ideas
- shows little evidence of voice, humor, individuality
- suggests a low-risk involvement by the writer (utterly safe idea, comments)

Reaching Writing: The writing reaches toward an audience.
- seems to move away from the concrete
- begins to elaborate on ideas, questions
- occasionally cites examples, supports ideas
- gives some sense of the author; voice beginning to emerge
- might relate an idea to an experience
- might be experimental, seeking a specific reader

Connecting Writing: The writing connects with the audience.
- has a sense of voice, a picture of the author emerges
- attempts to connect ideas, opinions, and emotions with experiences; tries to synthesize and/or analyze an idea
- might be an attempt at metaphor, simile, analogy, or illustrating an idea through a personal narrative
- might be an attempt to explain an idea or opinion through examples from the text

Striving Writing: The writing connects to the audience in an experimental, speculative, or thought-provoking manner.
- experiments with language: metaphor, analogy, humor, word play
- seems honest, sincere
- suggests a high level of risk taking
- provides genuine insight into the text, the writer's life, or life in general
- speculates and explores ideas and opinions

Talking Writing: The writing becomes a dialogue between writers.
- "sounds" like dialogue
- often includes direct questions and answers
- often asks for elaboration and clarification
- builds a conversation on previous talking writing
- refers to cultural, regional, and personal material not apparently related to the text
- frequently contains slang, humor, and a sense of playfulness

put things like pictures of my family like my brother, my sister, and my mom and dad, on my walls.

Rian Bristow, Talkeetna, Alaska

The first thing I would do is take a bath and then I would eat until I puked. Then I would go and have the time of my life.

Tom Chaffee, Corinth, Vermont

I would probably go to Barre with my older cousin and go the Mall and arcade, and get a sandwich at one of the restaurants.

Wayne Darling, Corinth, Vermont

These responses are similar in that they are one or two sentences in length and basically consist of a simple statement about what the student would do after coming out of hiding. There is no explicit connection with the diary and very little elaboration of the ideas. It is difficult to "see" these writers because of the perfunctory nature of their responses. Tom Chaffee's response is an example of what I refer to in the middle school classroom as a "statusizing act," an effort to attract attention by pushing the boundaries on what is acceptable. The student would probably be pleased in this case if the teacher came over and mentioned that "puked" wasn't appropriate. (I hope I don't sound overly critical of these responses.) As I mentioned earlier, there is no linear progression from one type of writing to another. In contrast to other responses, however, these seem to reflect a minimal investment by the writer.

In my classroom, these kinds of responses were frequently restating comments from class discussions. Although the "performing" responses tended to happen early on, they were present through the duration of the conference. I think this is due in part to the fact that all of us respond differently to different stimuli, not only in our writing, but in life. Some prompts elicited lively reactions from the third-hour students, while the same prompt resulted in sighs of boredom in the fourth-hour class. One of the things that I like about being a writing teacher, although it is frustrating at times, is that we are always standing on shifting ground. Our assumptions and our realizations are only as sound as the particular day or process in which they are enacted. We do learn and improve as we go. But there is never a surefire method, a fail-safe plan for making it all work as it should.

Reaching Writing: The writing reaches toward an audience

The second type of writing that occurred throughout the conference is referred to as "reaching writing." I think you can see in the next responses that the student is stepping out of the role of performing and is showing some purpose in his or her writing. This writing does not appear as self-conscious as the performing writing. The main differentiating characteristic between reaching writing and performing writing is that reaching writing begins to elaborate on ideas and opinions, and to ask rhetorical questions.

> I would be scared because I wouldn't know who was next. Would it be against my race or religion? The Jews didn't do anything, so why not take other innocent people too? If my parents agreed, I would take some Jews into my home, but it might be hard to stay friends with my Jewish friends because everyone would be saying bad things about them. It would be hard to do something on your own.
>
> Maria Heidenreich, Corinth, Vermont

This next response is an example of a student conceptualizing the issue, moving beyond the concrete, literal reply to abstract notions of religion and race. This writing moves the reader into the hypothetical situation through questions.

> If there are any Jewish kids there I would like to know what you think about Hitler. If you were a Jew who survived The Holocaust what do you feel and say to the outside world? If you were a German living in Germany would you tell or keep the secret if you were captured?
>
> Molly Preston, Corinth, Vermont

Clearly, this student is seeking a specific reader or group of readers. It is responses like this one that illustrate the power of posting writing in telecommunications conferences.

Through telecommunication conferences, students can ask specific questions to an audience holding diverse views and coming from different backgrounds, and they also can receive responses from these multiple perspectives. In contrast, the response journals that students typically do are two-dimensional: the student writes, and the teacher responds. Occasionally students write to each other, but this activity is limited. But, in telecommunications conferences, the student writes, a multitude of readers consider the writing, and some of these readers respond. Reaching writing sometimes acknowledges that there are many people reading the work.

> I can't move or walk around. I can't wait until later because I've got so much energy inside of me right now. Do my friends miss me? Have they been taken? I must never give up hope. That seems to be all there is left of me.
>
> Vekeesha, Guntown, Mississippi

To Jason Conaway . . . If I had to find a hiding place it would be in a tree in some woods where they would never look. I enjoyed learning about someone's whole life. *Do you think Anne was sad or happy to die when it came?*

Wayne Baker, Guntown, Mississippi

In the previous three responses, the students are asking questions of their readers, not merely returning the original question back to the reader, but inquiring about their opinions on matters relating to the issue, such as their emotional reactions. Although the last question probably occurred to many readers of the diary, it is the kind that is rarely voiced during a literary discussion in the middle school classroom. This kind of emotional, sympathetic query could be greeted with snickers or teasing from less-mature or less-sensitive classmates, but online the student can take this risk, because the student writer is not sitting in class with the person he or she is writing to, and doesn't have to encounter that person elsewhere in the school. The student is free to create a new "self" online, a very tempting proposition for an adolescent, and has an opportunity to try out some of the new insights and speculation gained about the world, and personally.

Erin Z., I agree with you. I can't talk to my parents or anyone I have to live with. I like to talk to my friends or my peers and I like to talk to my basketball coach or Mrs. Buse. I feel like my parents don't know what I am talking about.

Tiffany May, Guntown, Mississippi

Here, a student is writing directly to another student and explaining exactly what she thinks about the issue at hand, communicating with parents. It is an honest, straightforward reply, which cites examples and explains the reasons behind her opinion.

We think that we would go to the North pole and build igloos, have servants, and make them go back to Fairbanks and get us everything we needed. We would occasionally (VERY occasionally) have our parents fly up . We would have all of our pets and a big heater that won't melt ice.

Amy Dale, Jamie Carmon, Nikiski, Alaska

If I came out from hiding I would go out and smell fresh air and jump in the snow. I would play around that whole day enjoying the fresh air and what it feels like to be free. I would also go out and drive my snowmachine. I would drive to my friend's house and see if they could go riding (if they had a snowmachine).

Ryan Ellis, Nikiski, Alaska

Although each of the two preceding responses has a clear voice (as in Amy and Jamie's "VERY occasionally"), the last response has a lively and conversational voice, with phrases like "smell fresh air" and "what it feels like to be free." This writing has a tone of excitement and a clear purpose. There is also a movement in the response from the concrete/literal to the abstract notion of how all of us should live. The parenthetical phrase, designed to help the reader accurately picture the described event, further shows a sense of concern for the audience. This student didn't want readers in Mississippi to think that every home in Alaska had a snowmachine. There was a lively exchange early in the conference about what a snowmachine was (aka a snowmobile in the Lower Forty-Eight), how they were used, and so on. There was a roar of laughter in one of my classes when the question "What is a snowmachine?" was displayed by the overhead. Then there was a bewildered silence when I explained that there are adults living in the South who have never seen real snow. It was stranger than fiction to the young Alaskans.

In order to share the conference writing that came in from the other classrooms, I would download the writing onto my hard drive at home. The next morning I would print out the responses and make an overhead transparency. By using an overhead, my students and I could read the responses aloud together and discuss them. That format also made the conversations more public, and the kids were excited to see their names on the overhead. Since computer access was limited, and we didn't have modem access at school at that time anyway, it simply wasn't practical for kids to go online. I would also make several photocopied packets of the responses for the small groups and pairs to use as they drafted their responses.

> To Cara Honan, To me, Anne was not that conceited. She was just acting like an average thirteen-year-old girl. But she does change her views and her perspective about life. Later on she began thinking farther than just a couple days in the future. I believe she was a strong-hearted girl.
>
> Tammy Brown, Guntown, Mississippi

Throughout the conference, there were references to Anne. Anne Frank's articulate, at times poetic, voice was an integral part of the conversations, as well as a frequent subject. I often wondered if this conference would have exploded in the way that it did without the diary as a common text. My assumption is that there might have been the initial enthusiasm about the connection between classes, but it was the powerful reaction to the text that sustained the conference, the desire on the part of many students to process, to discuss, and to understand this disturbing and poignant story of someone very similar to themselves. One of the remarkable qualities of the diary, which sets it apart from novels and other works, is the progression that we see in terms of Anne's growing up, which we hear in her own words. The three "worlds" within the diary—Anne's thoughts and emotions, the world inside the Annex, and the world outside the Annex—are interwoven throughout the entries in a seemingly effortless structure designed to make sense of all three. It is this complexity, combined with the power and poetic qualities of Anne's writing, that works to affect young adults so powerfully. The statement "I believe she was a strong-hearted girl" in Tammy's piece is another example of a statement that might fit into the literary discussion in the classroom. Again we see a student reaching out to a reader.

Connecting Writing: The writing connects with the audience

In connecting writing we begin to sense contact between the reader and writer. By this, I mean that the writer seems to have a *specific* audience in mind, which is sometimes indicated by the start of the message, if it is addressed to a specific individual, or by its response to a specific piece of writing in the exchange. This is the category in which I think the writing begins to separate itself from what I typically see in the classroom. If I were to apply the "markers" of connecting writing as criteria to the writing I often see in response journals, I would find few examples. The key ingredient typically missing in classroom writing is the authentic audience.

With connecting writing, unlike so much of the writing I typically see in my classroom, the writing is *alive*. It is not the dull, colorless page filler that I often see. Here are several samples of the kind of writing from the first year of the conference that exhibit the traits I associate with connecting writing.

> To me life is like a puzzle and every day you add a piece to fit it together. You start it when you're born and complete it when you die.
>
> Jennifer Cyr, Corinth, Vermont

This metaphor might be overused, but when you think of it in the context of the story of Anne Frank, it is relevant. The idea that the pieces of Anne's puzzle were being determined by forces—inhumane forces—well beyond her control is poignant.

The next several responses are examples of writing with the distinct sound of the writer's voice. Certainly there is some subjectivity involved here, but I can see and "hear" these young writers as they respond to the prompts.

I wouldn't go into hiding because why should I have to suffer for standing up for what I believe in? I would feel my country betrayed me. If I had to hide, *I would feel lonely, insecure, and angry at the world.*

Tanya Tresino, Talkeetna, Alaska

Entry One: If I was in hiding for two years and I was able to go home, I would run outside and breathe the fresh air. I would scream my lungs out and run around. Then I would go home, take a shower (since I would probably smell pretty bad) and then pig out! I would call my friends, especially my best friend Jessica. Later on I would just look at my stuff in my bedroom and lie on my bed. I would just go to sleep.

Entry Two: If I was hiding and I got to put some stuff on my wall, I would put pictures of my friend, house, family, animals, so I could look at them all the time. Pictures of sports (volleyball, soccer, basketball). I would bring a bunch of my stuffed animals, because my family gave them to me and that would make me think of them.

Amy Hutchings, Nikiski, Alaska

I would, without a doubt, RUN . . . through the woods like a lunatic who has a problem keeping on his feet . . . I wouldn't sleep. So I'd find a place that prepares food and eat them out of business. Then after I am 41 and 1/16 lbs heavier and feeling sicker then a wet ham, I would roll to the nearest arcade and blow all the pocket change I'd collected over the years. *Now that I was poor, fat and fully rested, I would trek to my NEW home!*

Chris Emerson, Corinth, Alaska

If I got back at breakfast time I would have a humungous plate of home fries just dripping with ketchup. I would look for my animals. I would spend time sitting in my very own room, in my very own bed and petting my cat or at my barn with my horse. Then I know I would go outside and walk the trails near my house, through the woods and through the fields. *When I came to a sunny spot I would lie down in the grass and stare at the sky and clouds. All the while I would try to figure out what each cloud looked like to me.* Afterwards I would walk home to where my mom would have a beautiful lunch ready. I would call all my friends and go to the Panda house for Chinese dinner. I would go home and not be neat. I would not put my clothes away neatly . . . I would just throw them on the floor and get in my nightgown, jump in my bed and go to sleep . . . Happy.

Kate Martin, Corinth, Vermont

This student has transported herself from the classroom into the imagery of her writing. It seems as though she is imagining the words as she writes them, which gives the passage a certain immediacy and energy. I think it is safe to assume that she is imagining an audience for her writing as well. The response is clearly intended to be read and appreciated, *to communicate* with someone, not merely to be turned in and graded. This next response also displays the immediacy that I'm describing.

> Anne gets along better with her father than her mother, because her mother tries too hard to be her friend. Her mother, in Anne's eyes, is a strong person who likes her sister better than she likes Anne. It is just the same with me. I get along better with my dad than I do with my mom because my dad lets me get away with more stuff! My mom always wants to go by rules, and she never does anything fun and wild. My mom is gone a lot, so my dad and I joke around. *When my nineteen-year-old sister comes to visit, I feel like my mom enjoys being with her, more than with me. I talk to my mom about it and she doesn't understand. . . .*
>
> The main reason I think Anne and her mother don't get along very well, is because they are so much alike, that it make(s) them not get along. Her father and she have more things to talk about, because Anne finds cooking, cleaning, sewing, and the normal womanly jobs boring.
>
> I think Anne is conceited at the beginning of the book. She takes everything for granted until she goes into hiding. Then she becomes a different person.
>
> Even though Anne complains a lot in her diary about the people in the annex, I don't think she is conceited in any way when she goes into hiding. She has a right to privacy, and the other people in the annex do not give it to her.
>
> Sonja Frojen, Unalaska, Alaska

Frankly, I don't think many adult readers could write such a perceptive and concise analysis of Anne's character as Sonja has done. It wasn't until my second and third readings of the book that I began to understand the tensions between Anne and her mother.

The next piece typifies the kind of thoughtful, elaborate writing that came from Tom's classroom. Although we couldn't "see" the structure, the influence of the student-directed collaborative time and the fact that the students were older resulted in some great modeling of good writing for other students in the conference.

> *I think Anne gets along with her father better because Anne might remind her mother of what she was like when she was Anne's age.* Because that's how it is with me and my mom. When she was my age she wasn't as wild as I am, but she had the same attitude that I do and I guess that it is just hard for her to raise me sometimes because she sees herself. And she is afraid I'm going to get

into trouble like get pregnant or get into drugs real heavy or something like that, but she's starting to trust me more and more everyday which is real cool.

> Me and my dad get along great because I'm his only daughter and he really spoils me (my parents are divorced so I see him every third weekend of the month). But it's fun to be daddy's little girl, because he lets me do more things than my 16 year old brother. He is also getting me a car at age 14, cool huh? Well talk to you all later.

Rainy Richardson, Talkeetna, Alaska

The first sentence of this response is an insightful remark for an eighth grader (or any reader) to make regarding Anne and her father. It might be another example of using the book to understand your life, and your life to understand the book. Again, this student wants to explain to her audience what she has learned from the book and what it means in terms of her existence. It is also a seemingly honest piece of writing.

Students don't often volunteer information about divorces or step-parents. There is tremendous pressure to fit in and to be like everyone else. I am continually amazed by the openness and frank dialogue that happens in the Anne Frank Conference. That candor is evident in the following responses from the first year, during which (as in subsequent years) the topic of motherhood was a hot button for conversation.

> I think she likes her father more because he may pay more attention to her than her mother. Mr. Frank probably knows how Anne feels because Mrs. Frank acts the same way toward him. I like my mom more than my dad because my mom has been with me fourteen years of my life, and my dad never came around after they were divorced.

Brandy Malone, Guntown, Mississippi

> I believe a mother goes through almost everything a daughter does. She knows about her life stages and the problems with friends and other relationships. Fathers do not go through everything a girl does. A mother tries to butt in sometimes, but it's only normal. They worry a lot. They want to know about school and they worry about what the future will bring. Because her mother is always worrying. Anne feels close to her father because he allows her to be free.
>
> Later Gator,

Jessica May, Guntown, Mississippi

There is a simple beauty in this writing. The student is thinking seriously about an important issue, something she has obviously considered prior to writing. I see this piece in particular as being emblematic of the maturation that often takes place in eighth graders. Eighth graders generally enter the school year as awkward older children, displaying fumbling attempts at what they perceive to be grown-up behaviors and attitudes. But, as the year goes on, I occasionally see the beginnings of true adulthood in their writing, or in a comment in class, indicating that these young people are genuinely considering the views and emotions of the people around them. They begin to leave the concrete, "me-centered" world of the older child and enter into an existence where, often, they are almost too aware of the perceptions of other people regarding their own behavior. In the above piece, the writer has, perhaps for the first time, stepped into her parent's shoes not only to understand what is best for the child at the moment, but to grasp the essential nature of good parenting. Maybe this student was more mature than the average student when she entered the eighth grade; then again, the experience of reading and writing and connecting with other students possibly provided a nudge toward maturity.

A couple of weeks ago I was driving my middle school ski team home from a meet. I looked in the back of the van and saw two of my "coolest" boy skiers, each with a plastic toy tank in hand, making exploding noises and machine gunfire sounds as they aimed the tanks at each other on the top of the seat. A while later, I heard one of my girl skiers remark that the best time to go to the new McDonald's play land was late at night because you could play "when the little kids aren't there." All these students will be entering high school next year. It is observations like these, as well as the analysis of the kind of writing like Jessica's, that continually remind me that the social, psychological, physical, and emotional development that is happening with my students is directly related to, and probably the single strongest determining factor in, their literacy development as well. In the middle school, perhaps more than at any other level in education, these developmental processes overshadow any neat paradigms of literacy skill continuums. Students must reach a certain maturity level before they can write sincerely and thoughtfully without the "statusizing," posturing sorts of statements that are so common in the upper elementary grades. In fact, I would suggest that because of all of the emotional and psychological turmoil that kids are experiencing with puberty, it takes activities with real substance and issues that are immediately relevant to the kids to even *begin to get their attention* away from social concerns.

4 Exchanging Lives: Talking Writing

I've learned that we live on a seesaw. On one end we are alike, but on the other end we differ. It's so amazing to feel that there are people hundreds or thousands of miles away that we might know, but we don't know them at all. Peoples lives, speech, homes, hobbies are so different in Mississippi and Alaska from Vermont.

Nathaniel Maxwell, Corinth, Vermont

The preceding comment reflects the sentiments of many of the students who participated in the online exchange of the Anne Frank Conference the first three years of its existence. This writing suggests to me what is most crucial about why these exchanges should happen. Certainly, they encourage students to learn to read more critically and to write more clearly with a purpose and audience in mind. But perhaps a greater benefit is that students are forced to examine their lives, their schools, and their communities through the eyes of students from around the country; they come to see where they have common ground and where they differ, an experience that is difficult to bring about in the traditional isolated classroom. One of the reasons students have been willing to share so openly has been the mode of communication that emerged in the conference. Despite having closely observed adolescents in my classroom and in a variety of nonacademic settings, I had never seen this sort of literacy before. This mode of discourse, "talking writing," is utterly unique.

Although all the writing that has happened in the conference is "talking writing" in one sense (because it is more "verbal" than most of the writing that we see in the classroom), there have been certain instances when a dialogue emerged between students. This kind of writing does not happen anywhere else. When kids write notes to each other in class, or write to each other in dialogue journals, or respond to each other's writing in response groups, they don't have the cultural and regional differences the students in the exchange had, and that they wanted to bridge with their writing. There is something compelling for students to be connected to other young people in different locations. Part of it is a curiosity about other people; it is also a desire to explain themselves, to make a statement about who they are as they discover themselves. As we look at examples of this kind of writing, in which the students spontaneously engaged in direct conversations with each other, the energy and dynamic nature of the communication comes to life. Having the text as a center for discussion allowed students to experiment with the mode of communication, and the conversation quickly broadened as the connections became more direct, until the students were virtually in the same room with each other, creating a powerful social connection through their writing. It was through the striving and talking writing that students were able to make this project their own and to truly attempt to make meaning, free of any teacher-imposed constraints or predispositions. At times, the teachers felt like mere tools in the machinery of the exchange, and the technology became invisible. I remember Peggy Turner writing about feeling as if she were being dragged down the hallway by her hair in order to transmit the students' writing. That's power!

Talking Writing: The writing becomes a dialogue between writers

Of all the categories, there is the most overlap between striving writing (to be discussed in Chapter 5) and talking writing, primarily because both demonstrate a real connection with a reader. The distinction that I made in looking at these two types of writing was whether or not the response was *specifically* addressed to another student, or was obviously in reply to another student's writing. Observed that way, talking writing:

- "sounds" like dialogue
- often includes direct questions and answers
- often asks for elaboration and clarification
- builds a "conversation" on previous talking writing
- refers to cultural, regional, and personal material not apparently related to the text
- frequently contains slang, humor, and a sense of playfulness

I'd like to begin this section with an excerpt from an exchange between Ryan L'herlaut from Sondra Porter's class and my students in Nikiski. It began with our prompt: "If you went into hiding, where would you go?" Here is Ryan's reply:

> If I had to go into hiding in Talkeetna I would just go for a really long walk in the woods with a pack, tent, gun, sleeping bag, bul-

lets, a knife, matches, lighters, a sled and dogs (to eat) to pull the sled. Then I would just continually move and hope I never got caught.

Ryan L'herlaut, Talkeetna, Alaska

I recall reading this reply to my students from the overhead and their immediate disgust for eating dogs. It should also be noted that this reply is an example of the many regional differences that emerged. There was no mention of dogsleds from the kids in Mississippi. Here are a few replies to his message.

To: Ryan L'heraut, Su-Valley
From: Jeremy Russell, Nikiski, Alaska
Subject: Your dogs

I think you're pretty disgusting if you would eat your dogs after they practically saved your life. Also, if you had a sled you could have loaded a bunch of dehydrated foods for yourself. The dogs could also work for you out there.

To: Ryan L'herlaut, Su-Valley
From: Melissa Bradley, Nikiski, Alaska
Subject: Killing Your Dogs!

Why would you want to eat your dogs? Your dogs are working hard for you. Plus, if you're bringing a knife, gun and matches you can kill other animals besides your dogs.

To: Ryan L'herlaut, Su-Valley
From: Gloria Hollingsworth, Nikiski, Alaska
Subject: Hiding

You know, I don't think I would eat the dogs, but I like your idea about going into the woods and I hope I wouldn't get caught. But, I think I might bring some food.

After receiving a multitude of lively responses addressed to him, Ryan then responded to his readers.

To: All those who were totally disgusted that I might eat my dogs

About the dogs . . . I wouldn't actually eat my dogs unless I was starving, and even then I wouldn't enjoy it (unless they were really spicy). I really like dogs. I have a mastiff (English of course.) , and a Sharpei. The mastiff lives here in Alaska with me and I have the Sharpei in British Columbia (where I spend my summers). I'm not that great of a hunter and I'd rather eat dog than starve. After all they eat dog in some countries, so it wouldn't kill me unless I ate the liver. A few famous expedition members over the years have died from eating their dogs' livers to keep from starving. One of these was the Franklin Expedition.

Ryan L'herlaut, Talkeetna, Alaska

This exchange reflected many of the characteristics of what I'm referring to as talking writing. The writing "sounds" like dialogue. I could imagine the three Nikiski students asking their questions just as they are written in a small group setting. There are direct questions and answers, as well as elaboration and clarification (Ryan's last response), and the conversation builds on previous writing. Also, the writing refers to cultural, regional, and personal material, not apparently related to the text (the Mastiff, the Sharpei, and summers in British Columbia). And clearly, there is humor and a sense of playfulness: "unless they were really spicy." Here the kids are being themselves. It often takes extraordinary effort for some eighth graders to remain serious, even about matters of life and death—perhaps especially in dealing with matters of life and death—for any length of time. The fact that humor appears here is an indication to me of the genuine nature of the writing. (Speaking of humor, I have some boys this year who specialize in producing giggles and guffaws in my second-period class. The next exchange features some of their goofiness.)

At this point I'd like to make a few comments on the reaction to the book in general. I can't emphasize enough the power of the Anne Frank diary as the central focus point in the exchange. We've learned through BreadNet that meaningful exchanges can happen in a variety of formats, focusing on a wide range of texts and issues. But a crucial element is the link between the central text and the student participants.

I hope that I haven't given the impression in this book that all of the eighth graders who read *Anne Frank: The Diary of a Young Girl*, or the dramatized version, were swept away or captivated by this important literary work. In fact, in most classrooms there is resistance to the book, especially early on, and particularly from male students. For one thing, the book was not written as a novel, nor was it intended to be read or published. It is a struggle for readers to leave behind the traditional reader's paradigm of the sequential narrative in order to get into the rhythm of the diary. Also, the book is almost an antithesis to so much of the young adult pulp fiction on the market, such as that written by Christopher Pike, R. L. Stine, and others, whose only intent is to keep the reader turning pages.

The diary is the creation of an introspective, poetic, literary mind. For students to step into this world, they have to be grounded in the basic history of the period, and they have to leave behind their expectations as readers. For most kids, the idea of sitting down to write about important issues like war, love, nature, and God, as Anne did, is as foreign as performing brain surgery, and just as appealing. Here is a diary entry from Wednesday, February 23, 1944:

> A thought:
>
> We miss so much here, so very much and for so long now; I miss it too, just as you do. I'm not talking of outward things, for we are looked after in that way; no, I mean the inward things. Like you, I long for freedom and fresh air, but I believe now that we have ample compensation for our privations. I realized this quite suddenly when I sat in front of the window this morning. I mean inward compensation.
>
> When I looked outside right into the depth of Nature and God, then I was happy, really happy. And Peter, so long as I have that happiness here, the joy in nature, health and lot more besides, all the while one has that, one can always recapture happiness.
>
> Riches can all be lost, but that happiness in your own heart can only be veiled, and it will still bring you happiness again, as long as you live. As long as you can look fearlessly up into the heavens, as long as you know that you are pure within and that you will still find happiness . . .

This passage is only a portion of more than two hundred pages of Anne's thoughts. At first, many students may think she wrote the way she did because she lived in a different age, when young people were supposed to be like that. However, as they get to know her and to grow with her, many students—and teachers—come to the realization that Anne was not merely a victim of the Holocaust, whose diary survived as a testament to the atrocities that occurred, but a gifted writer and thinker in her own right. In terms of relating the preceding passage to the present day, I think that, rather unfortunately, we live in a society where young people are trained to anticipate immediate material rewards for their labors. The idea of learning for the sake of learning, a value that Anne demonstrated arduously, is a totally new concept for many students. As students begin to read the entries in the diary, and discover that there is very little physical action (unlike the novels, movies, and television shows they are so accustomed to), they complain that the book is boring. Usually, most students move beyond this, as they get to know Anne and her family and empathize with the difficulty of her situation. There is also some fairly difficult vocabulary in the diary, as seen in the previous entry. (Later, I'll present a letter from Phil Sittnick discussing his concern about this initial reaction.)

The next writing is an early portion from the third year of the exchange that shows students talking about this issue, and themselves, and getting their feet wet regarding the whole idea of telecommunications. The first piece, by Ryan, is a typical early response from the conference. He is answering the questions, "performing" as he is expected to do. However, the responses *to* his writing are what I would consider talking writing. This talking writing feels like the kind of talk you would expect if some teenagers met each other in the bleachers for a game, or while waiting in line for a movie ticket.

> Hi, my name is Ryan Aragon and I am an eighth grader at Laguna Middle school. I am going to answer the questions you sent about Anne Frank. To question number 1, I think Anne wants to be like her sister because she wants to stay out of trouble and be more responsible. I would like to be like Anferne Hardaway and play on the Bulls NBA team because he has more skills and talent in basketball and also I want to be rich. Now question number 2. If I had just gotten out I would get some new clothes especially and then get some food to eat. What I feel about this book, I think it's boring because she keeps talking about things in the past which I really ain't into a lot, and she just tells what happened each day and how she feels. I really can't relate to what she is talking about.

> Ryan,
>
> Yo! This is a group consisting of four guys, as you can read by our names. We read that you'd like to play basketball with the Bulls when you're older. Our high school's teams, both guys' and girls', just won the state tourney! Although this is a nice little sport, it is comparatively wimpy to the popular sport of snowshoe karate, played in boxer shorts during sub-zero conditions (just jokin').
>
> We agree that it's kind of dull (the book), but you hafta remember that it was a Jewish girl's diary and she never meant for it to be published, or even read by someone else. Even so, she's a pretty good writer.
>
> Till the next time,
> Four spiffy, neat-o, really cool Alaskans
>
> From: Tony Mika, Dylan Smith, Donnie Euper, and Mario Bird, Nikiski, Alaska

> Dear Ryan;
>
> We feel the exact same way you do, we do not like the book. But Casey does not want to be Anfernee. Jeremy likes Anfernee but

Michael Jordan is better. Jeremy is really sad right now because his igloo just melted down because we had a tropical heat wave. Just kidding! We don't live in igloos. We live in normal houses. You know what? They should just let the Bulls take the championship now before all of the teams in their path get slaughtered.

From: Casey Heath, Jeremy Vance, and Gabe Segura, Nikiski, Alaska

To: Ryan Aragon

Hi Ryan! We do not live in igloos, just so you know! We are all girls except for James. What is pizza? We have never had it up here. We only eat whale and walrus meat. JUST KIDDING!! We do have pizza and we don't eat walrus and whale meat! Anyway, we got your response about Anne Frank and you wanting to play basketball for the Bulls and wanting to be rich. We all want to be rich too!

If we were to just get out of hiding, James says he would walk through the woods with his dog. Kim would go walk in the woods and scream as loud as she could. Randee and I (Valerie) would too. Well, we gotta go now so please write us back!

From: Kim Lynch (age 13), Randee Wilson (age 14), James Broussard (age 13), Valerie Hicks (age 14), Nikiski, Alaska

These messages do not contain brilliant insights into the nature of life as an eighth grader, nor into the diary. But it is real writing with a purpose, about things that are important to the kids . . . basketball, getting rich, and some kidding around about life in Alaska. With six exclamation points in one message (above) there must be a certain enthusiasm for the writing.

Before we look at a few more specific back-and-forth exchanges, here are a few exchanges of talking writing from the first year of the conference. The first message is a poignant reminder that many people are still living with the effects of World War II more than fifty years after it ended.

About WWII

My Grampa on my mom's side was in WWII. He is so messed up because of it. Anytime he watches a movie or hears about the war, he freaks out. For example, he watched "The Posse" and for about a week he was silent. He had nightmares and was just not himself. Grampa was also exposed to mustard gas and ever since then he hasn't been able to walk right. Most of his friends also have problems similar to his. They all want to do something about it, but what can they do?

Jamie Sampson, Corinth, Vermont

There were several students in different classes who wrote about their grandfather's experiences in World War II and their lingering effects. These stories impacted other students who then responded. The following response from a student in Sondra Porter's class was typical of the inquiries that came back:

> To Jamie Sampson
>
> Your Grandpa must have had a bad time in the war to have nightmares and stuff like that. I have heard of Mustard gas but I am not sure what it does. I just know that you could die from it. Because your story was interesting we talked about Mustard gas in our science class today. My science teacher thought that it burnt your skin and since they did not have any antibiotics it also infected your skin and you could die from the infection.
>
> Obviously that didn't happen to your Grandfather.
>
> What did your Grampa do in the war, and what was his rank? I really like your story. It was really written good.
>
> Rian Bistow, Talkeetna, Alaska

This message gave one example of the many tangential learning activities that the conference inspired. For instance, many students, even in Alaska, did not know that the Japanese invaded, and actually occupied part of, Alaska for a brief time during World War II.

Sometimes the online "conversations" took place over several weeks, as students wrote their responses, teachers posted them on BreadNet, the next class read them and responded, and so on. Although it was much more immediate than the "snail mail" exchanges through the post office, there was a delay between responses. The following exchange began with Dan's comments on February 8, continued with Jamie's response on February 16, and concluded with Rainy's response, posted on March 1.

> I think Anne gets along better with her father because he is not always giving her a hard time and making her miserable. I side with my mom a lot more than my dad because she's not so demanding and tries to make things easier.
>
> Dan Clark, Talkeetna, Alaska

> I feel the same way as Dan Clark does, that Anne gets along better with her father because he is more lenient towards Anne than her mother. I think her mother expects more from Anne and expects her to be perfect.

Myself, I am the same way as Anne because I get along better with my father because of my various interests, but both parents are hard on me when it comes to schooling and education.

Jamie Claflin, Corinth, Vermont

To Jamie Claflin,

I like everything you wrote about, because I agree with it all. The part about how you get along better with your father than your mother. It's the same way for me too. I don't know what it is but me and my dad get along so much better. We have the same points about everything that has to do with life and growing up while my mom and I have the totally opposite opinions about life and growing up. Both my parents are also very hard on me when it comes to education and schooling.

I think it would be very hard to live with Mr. and Mrs. Van Daan because I just can't stand people like them telling what to do, how to act, giving me lectures, I don't really think it would be that hard to live with Mrs. Frank because my mom is kinda like her and I have lived with my mom except for one year (family problems.)

I think it would be very hard to live with someone I loved as a boyfriend. It would be very hard to do that because when I'm going out with people I usually like to be alone and just spend time with that person, and it would be hard to do so because that place was so small.

I have also learned a lot from the telecommunications and I hope I can learn some things because this is fun writing to people and getting things back. Well talk to ya all later. It's been fun writing

Rainy Richardson, Talkeetna, Alaska

Perhaps Rainy's reply is stretching it a bit in terms of its classification as talking writing. It does come closer to the sound and length of a letter. But I think she had a lot to say and was clearly "talking" to someone in particular. The fact that she was willing to talk about boyfriends and "family problems," even in passing, suggests that she is not addressing the world at large.

I don't think telecommunications is the only factor inspiring the students to write openly and sincerely. In a sense, Anne Frank's diary is a form of talking writing, in that she has a very specific reader in mind (Kitty) and that the writing sounds verbal. It's important for Anne to enter the conversation here so we can hear the words that fueled the debate about motherhood, and hear the voice of the young woman whose growing up has become a force in the lives of millions of young readers. Although she didn't have a modem, Anne Frank was very much a part of this conference, from modeling good writing to bringing an introspective, self-critical, literary, and (at times) poetic view of the world to the students involved.

> Sunday, January 2, 1944
>
> Dear Kitty,
>
> This morning when I had nothing to do I turned over some of the pages of my diary and several times I came across letters dealing with subject "Mummy" in such a hotheaded way that I was quite shocked, and asked myself " Anne, is it really you who mentioned hate? Oh Anne, how could you!" I remained sitting with the open page in my hand, and thought about it and how it came about that I should have been so brimful of rage and really so filled with such a thing as hate that I had to confide it all in you. I have been trying to understand the Anne of a year ago and to excuse her, because my conscience isn't clear as long as I leave you with these accusations, without being able to explain, on looking back how it happened.
>
> I suffer now—and suffered then—from moods which kept my head under water (so to speak) and only allowed me to see the things subjectively without enabling me to consider quietly the words of the other side, and to answer them as the words of one whom I, with my hotheaded temperament, had offended or made unhappy . . .
>
> I used to be furious with Mummy, and still am sometimes. It's true that she doesn't understand me, but I don't understand her either. She did love me very much and she was tender, but as she landed in so many unpleasant situations through me, and was nervous and irritable because of other worries and difficulties, it is certainly understandable that she snapped at me.

After reading this passage from Anne Frank's diary, it is remarkable to me that students thousands of miles away and five decades later are coming to similar realizations regarding their interactions with their parents. Through reflection and self-analysis, they are becoming adults, aware not only of their own motivations and foibles but of those of the people around them.

The following exchange was initiated when a student wrote that he would hide in a copper mine and one of my classes asked for more information. It is another example of a talking writing trait: a reference to regional and cultural information.

About the Copper Mines in Vermont:
I live about 1.5 miles from the copper mines. The copper mines have 13 caves including air vents. The streams all around them don't have any fish or animals living in them like all the other ones, because the copper kills the wildlife. The cave I went into (and where I'd hide if I had to) was about 15 feet high and 30 feet long. Then there was a small air vent. You can take copper rocks home. They got the copper out by railroad and little carts. There are still some carts in there. You can see remains of where the miners slept and had fireplaces. The only kind of animals that hang around up there are coyotes. The copper mines are no longer in use. They were done mining them out in between 1900's and 1920. No one is supposed to go up or be near the copper mines because they say they're burning up underneath the earth.

Dean Rominger, Corinth, Vermont

To: Dean Rominger, Vermont:
Wow! I think it would be interesting and fun to hide in the copper mines. But where would you get your food from? Wouldn't it be too big though? What would you bring with you? Wouldn't it be frightening to be there alone with all the bombing? Would you bring your friends or family or both? What about first aid? Would you bring a headset to listen to music? If you did get food then how would you cook it? Do you know how to cook?

Matt Mallory, Talkeetna, Alaska

Another exchange dealt with perceptions of regional differences. Here, one student raises and another one dispels the stereotyped images of Alaska and Alaskans, as seen in a popular television show.

Dear Alaskans,

My father was born in California, but as a child he was raised in Alaska. He talks about moving back up there. Where would be the most ideal place to live? I love mountains and oceans and where I live there are neither. I watch "Northern Exposure" a lot. Are things like that where you live?

Russell Cox, Guntown, Mississippi

Dear Russell Cox,

Life in Alaska is nothing, I repeat nothing like Northern Exposure! We do not live in igloos either, and we don't play baseball in the snow (and all of that stuff!) What is it like having Christmas without snow? I can't imagine it. It just wouldn't be the same. Tell Rebecca Hi. I would like to meet her. Warning: Don't come to Alaska, you wouldn't like it. Do any of you play hockey?

Adam Knudsen, Nikiski, Alaska

The following message from Twyla, which we will look at again in Chapter 5 at as an example of striving writing, initiated another conversation between students.

> After being in hiding for two years, once I got out I would probably still be paranoid to go outside, especially after a war. But I would want to see all my friends. Talk with them and go out to dinner, play basketball and go bowling at the Fishing-N-Bowl.
>
> You see, where I live we don't have any malls, fast food, or anything like that. We have beautiful nature, two grocery stores, and school and a bowling alley.
>
> Today is the 27th of January and it is so beautiful outside with perfect skiing snow. *The sun makes the bay sparkle with the reflection of the nearby mountains on it. And surprisingly there is no wind! I was just thinking how wonderful it would be to come out of hiding on this day.*
>
> Twyla Schasteen, Unalaska, Alaska

> Twyla, Love your name! I think it is very weird not to have a mall or Taco Bell. What do ya'll do? Never mind, I already know the answer. You ride snowmachines. Doesn't everyone in Alaska? In a way I would love to live up there because it seems so quiet and peaceful. Y'all must have a major small town. We have like tons of grocery stores and schools, etc. Keep on snowmachining! (Here we say keep on truckin')
>
> Katie Ellis, Guntown, Mississippi

It is truly amazing when you think about what has just happened in the preceding conversation. A girl in a remote Alaskan town is "talking" with a student in Mississippi after reading a common text. In a sense, they are seated around a literary dinner table, three thousand miles in diameter, speaking, joking, face-to-face. Does anyone else imagine a phone next to Katie's ear as she says, "Y'all must have a major small town"?

During the second year of the conference, I asked my students to respond in groups to the prompt from Mary Burnham's class, the Waits River Road Runners: "If you had lived in Nazi Germany, would you have hidden Jews in your home?" The replies to this prompt were surprising in their honesty. After a lively discussion, in which they couldn't reach consensus, the students in one of my groups opted to reply individually, instead of drafting a collaborative response.

> To the Road Runners,
>
> If we lived in Nazi Germany we would let people live with us depending on who they were. Joel wouldn't let them live with him unless they had a good place to hide.

Poppi: I wouldn't want to see them suffer, it was a dangerous time and I could probably get killed for keeping them, but I would sacrifice my freedom for someone to be saved from the murderous world that surrounds them.

Rebecca: I would house them even if I could die, because concentration camps were probably really bad. I wouldn't want to see anyone suffer.

Joel: I wouldn't hide anyone because I would be scared for my own life. Inside I would like to, but I know if it really happened, I wouldn't. (I feel terrible about it.)

Poppi Multz, Rebecca Hulien, Joel Gennari, Nikiski, Alaska

A few days later the responses came in from other classes. Not surprisingly, several were addressed to Joel.

To Joel Gennari: "When I heard Mrs. Burnham (my teacher) read your thoughts about hiding a Jew in your home, I personally thought that you sounded selfish and not very sensitive to anyone else's feelings, BUT as I read on I really did understand how you felt and what you meant by not knowing if you would hide a Jew because you would be putting your own life in danger. I would like to think and believe that I would hide a Jew. I feel terrible because I have two best friends who are Jewish and if the war was going on now, I would definitely hide them.

Karen Chicoine, Corinth, Vermont

To Joel:

I think that I probably agree with you. I say this because judging from the pictures and stories, I would rather not take the risk of going to a concentration camp myself. I wouldn't hide a Jew because the Germans kept excellent records. Therefore, they would know if a Jew was missing and they would start searching. If I was harboring that Jew and they found out I would most likely be sent with the Jew to a camp.

Carson Henry, Corinth, Vermont

Joel Gennari: I admire you for being honest about what you would do. Reading this book it seems like taking a Jew in would be the only right thing to do, although I am not sure if I would actually hide a Jew. I wish I could be 1000% sure that I would hide someone . . . but I can't.

Flora Cilley, Corinth, Vermont

Joel Gennari: I agree with you. I don't think I would have hidden Jews because if I got caught I would be in the same position as them. I don't like to sound cold, but if a German soldier said "Tell me where some Jews are hiding, or you die," I would probably tell.

                                                                    John Swantak

When we talked about our responses before sending them off, Joel was openly criticized by other members of the class for his response. The class was very much caught up in the spirit of heroism and overcoming evil. It was a vindication for Joel when the responses came in from the other classes. Again, if the students in the previous exchange had been seated around a table, their written comments could have been spoken just as easily.

The following exchange is truly one of substance. It began when Megan Ales responded to the second Nikiski prompt, during the second year of the conference. I wrote this prompt after taking notes during one of our class discussions:

> Nikiski Prompt:
>
> It was mentioned that there was some discussion of whether or not Anne was conceited or arrogant last week. This only fueled the debate here. When we talked about a prompt for this week, the class felt strongly that this was an issue that needed to be explored. But it would also be interesting to find out what the perceptions are out there regarding the changes that are happening in terms of Anne's outlook on life. After a full year in captivity, we begin to see a very different Anne than the young girl we met at the beginning of the book. How is she different? How is her life, outlook, personality similar to your own, or to that of people you know?

Here is Megan's response:

> I think Anne's life is a lot like mine. I have fights with my mom, but wouldn't everyone, because of being trapped in the annex for fifteen months? Whenever my parents are home I try to act like I can come back with something smart when they say something. Anne's personality has changed a lot. She went from being a chatterbox to almost saying nothing except to Peter. I think Anne was pretty brave not to say something to Mr. Van Daan when he was mean to her.
>
> Megan Ales, Corinth, Vermont

As I've mentioned previously, it is difficult for eighth graders to write analytically about literature; such analysis is often foreign to their experience. Compare the use of language in response to a work of literature to the language children are accustomed to: language for play, language to communicate their needs, language to express their learning, and so forth. Students do not bring much experience in the analysis of complex ideas and experiences with them to the middle school. Although I do think that students have experience in complex thinking outside of school, they are not accustomed to expressing these views and ideas. When this lack of experience is coupled with the void in meaningful, deliberate expression and analysis of ideas during school, it is no surprise that a teacher rarely encounters the kind of explication and analysis present in the next response. Its young writer, Christy, is using her experiences in life to understand the people in the book, and their experiences to understand her own. She then takes those ideas and shares them with a specific reader, a new friend in Vermont.

> This is in regards to the comments from Megan Ales. Your comments really interested me. I have the same feeling. I am the youngest child in my family. My mother and I never see eye to eye. We always argue over the smallest things. I have only one older sister and they get along as if they were best friends. But, on the other hand, there has always been a special bond between my father and me. This is the only comparison I have recognized between my life and Anne's.
>
> In one specific part of the book (p. 39) Anne brings up the relationships in the family. She makes the remark that her father and mother never rebuke her sister, Margot, but they always drop everything on her. She states that she feels miserable, taken for granted and judged unjustly. In my home, there are many of the same conflicts. I have an older sister, Amy, who is twenty and is still living at home. I agree that my mother has made many mistakes with me as she did with Amy. As I get older, I am beginning to understand the meaning of what my mother is trying to say. It's starting to prove to me that my mother cares enough to correct my mistakes and even my faults.
>
> Christy Boutwell, Juneau, Alaska

Megan then replies to Christy.

> Megan Ales to Christy Boutwell in Miss.: I don't think I understand my mother and how she wants me to act like my brother. To me he is a "freak"!! . . . but sometimes he is really cool and I like hanging out with him and his friends. My mom does correct every little thing I do, like Mrs. Frank does to Anne. Do you feel like sometimes you want to just give up and have everyone just leave you alone so you can go and figure things out? Anne could hardly have time to be by herself. I think that's what she used the writing in her Diary for.

Two students in Nikiski also chose to respond to Megan.

> Dear Megan Ales:
>
> Yes, I do, (think Anne's life is a lot like mine), but my mother never tells us that we have to act more like our brothers or sisters. And, our mothers always correct us on everything we say or do.

(I wish I could include a few responses from some of the mothers discussed here!)

> Dear Megan Ales: I think Anne's life is like my sister's. The only thing is that she fights with her dad and probably because she used to be cooped up with my dad and me for a long time. When she was as little as Anne, she used to write in her diary just like Anne (I should have read it!) She also used to do work in books and read all the time. She also had many boyfriends and still does. My sister got more and more mature, just like Anne. I don't know if she has read Anne's diary, but if she does, I hope she likes it better than me, because I don't really like the whole idea of reading a strange girl's diary.
>
> Wesley Fogle, Nikiski, Alaska

At this point in the school year, Wesley had been in my classroom for six months, and this is the first time that he mentioned his sister.

Students are often conditioned in our schools to leave their personal lives at home, unfortunately, and to concentrate instead on filling in blanks and bubbles and on memorizing facts. It seems that students like Megan, Christy, and Wesley frequently are waiting for an opportunity to discuss their lives outside of school, to make sense of this world and the people who are important to them. This talking writing allows some distance, in that it is not immediate. Students can think, reflect, compose, and revise (to a limited degree) before they send their writing. When the responses come back, there is time to think, unlike verbal conversation where the responses are immediate. Also, as we've discussed earlier, since the students in the exchange are not sitting in the same class, there is a certain security in their openness.

In this chapter we've looked at nine excerpts of conversations from the three years that the Anne Frank Conference has been in existence. The topics in these conversations have included: dog teams (survival in the wilderness), negative reactions to the book, the NBA, people living with the effects of World War II, getting along with parents and siblings, the copper mines of Vermont, bad television shows, a moral dilemma (hiding Jews), and a thoughtful discussion of how students' lives are similar to Anne's. This spontaneous diversity is the essence of the process through which students are, in effect, exchanging lives through telecommunications. They have created their own mode of discourse, or literacy, to facilitate the connection. As a teacher, I see this development in my classroom as nothing short of revolutionary.

5 When the Writing Matters: Striving Writing

Every English teacher cherishes those moments when students experiment with language and genuinely attempt to say something in a new or interesting way. While reading the responses in the transcript of the Anne Frank Conference, there were several times when I stopped and read the writing again so I could take a closer look at how powerfully the students had connected with the reader. When other teachers looked through sample pages from the transcript and labeled several responses using the taxonomy in Chapter 3, there were some categorizing discrepancies between "reaching" and "connecting" writing; however, whenever the teachers came across any writing sample that is included in this chapter, that writing was consistently designated as "striving writing."

Striving Writing: The writing connects to the audience in an experimental, speculative, or thought-provoking manner

I use this category to describe the occasional lightning bolt of inspiration, the dazzling moment when the stars are aligned just so, and a young writer finds the right words to create something unique and powerful. Or, as is often the case with good writing, the words come together to create a simple, straightforward message from the heart. Striving writing:

- experiments with language: metaphor, analogy, humor, word play
- seems honest, sincere
- suggests a high level of risk taking
- provides genuine insight into the text, the writer's life, or life in general
- speculates and explores ideas and opinions

I think it's best here to let the student writing speak for itself. As always, I give my ritual disclaimer: my selection of the following pieces as examples of striving writing is based on my experiences as a reader, writer, and teacher. Until Bill Gates comes up with Microsoft English Teacher, or any program that consistently evaluates and responds to student writing effectively, my package of skills, experiences, likes, and dislikes, packed onto the sectors on my crowded little hard drive, will have to suffice.

> I would feel all alone, like you had to hide from the world. If part of the world did not like my religion and forced my kind to be killed, *I would have a hungry feeling.* I would be afraid of everybody that saw me. I would miss my friends. People turned on each other just because someone said you cannot like a person because of religion. To not see daylight until you were in a different country, to feel like the world doesn't like you anymore would be terrifying. To hear that people are out looking for me to kill me would almost make me think I didn't belong. To think I was born on this earth to be different in a bad way would be horrible. It would make me depressed—ready to give up everything.
>
> Krystal Garcia, Talkeetna, Alaska

> *I would feel like a caterpillar trapped inside of a tightly closed jelly jar* hardly being able to breathe from the small holes that allow me such a small freedom. I need the cool breeze and warm sunshine to inspire me to go on living. I would surely go mad or maybe even die of loneliness.
>
> Shanna Duggar, Guntown, Mississippi

> After being in hiding for two years, once I got out I would probably still be paranoid to go outside, especially after a war. But I would want to see all my friends. Talk with them and go out to dinner, play basketball and go bowling at the Fishing-N-Bowl.
>
> You see, where I live we don't have any malls, fast food, or anything like that. We have beautiful nature, two grocery stores, and school and a bowling alley.
>
> Today is the 27th of January and it is so beautiful outside with perfect skiing snow. *The sun makes the bay sparkle with the reflection of the nearby mountains on it. And surprisingly there is no wind! I was just thinking how wonderful it would be to come out of hiding on this day.*
>
> Twyla Schasteen, Unalaska, Alaska

There are few things more dreary than the writing that often appears after a lesson about "descriptive writing." Many writing textbooks that are full of exercises to provoke good sensory details and colorful adjectives may end up encouraging trite, wordy, convoluted passages that are devoid of meaning and purpose. In Twyla's piece (also discussed in the last chapter), we not only get a vivid picture of the place where she lives, but her relationship to that place. Rural kids rarely get an opportunity in school to talk about their community or their neighborhood because everyone already knows about it. Through an experience like this, students have an opportunity to see their communities and their relationship to their community in a new light.

> My walls would have pictures and things that are dear to me. Photographs of the life I once knew. Perhaps a picture of my dog, Rufus, or my cat Blackie. Pictures of my house and yard to imagine that I am still there. Also pictures of movie stars to pretend that I am still in the "theater going life." Letters from special people, that I have collected through the years and have been thrown in a shoe box at the bottom of my drawer, would now come out and would help decorate my room. Pictures drawn and painted by my eccentric sister would also be displayed. Would we be together? If not, pictures of her (which were sent to me from college) would totally cover the walls. *Her red hair, slightly parted in the middle, with her warm melting smile would be able to make anyone wake cheerfully.*
>
> Jim Broutzos, Corinth, Vermont

> I'd have posters of famous people that I like as role models and pictures of my family, friends and comic book characters. I really love comic books and love to draw comics. I would go to my favorite place . . . the movies. *I would visit most of my friends and go out in the woods in a space I cleared out 'specially for just lingering. It's by a stream and the sound of the calm water trickling soothes my brain, leaving it open for more thoughts to get in.*
>
> Miah Johnson, Corinth, Vermont

> Is Anne conceited, arrogant: yes, I think so, at least in the beginning. She spends a lot of time before she and her family go into hiding talking about boys, courting and stuff like that. She was 'superficial' around her friends and in her writing. Anne hardly ever looked any further than a few days ahead of her.
>
> *But then she changes her views after they've been hiding for a while. She starts thinking less about material things and more about subjects that really matter. It seems that she gets to know her dad and herself better, reality, I guess, became more real to her.* I also think she was much more happy that way too.
>
> Cara Honan, Unalaska, Alaska

> At my house my mom works three jobs. She works at Lucky Star during the week and at another store she half owns. On Saturday she helps an old woman at her house. So I don't get to talk to my mom too much. We fuss like any other mother and son would. *For a couple of weeks now we have been fussing about which parent I want to stay with. I want to go move to my dad's house, but I*

feel sorry for my mom. She has raised me up since I was born. She thinks I don't know that but I do. Well, I don't need to get into my family problems right now. It is hard to bring friends to my house because I have a crippled sister named Tasha. She is ten. She was born with a disease that I cannot write the name of on the paper.

Anonymous, Guntown, Mississippi

One of the things that most frustrates me as a teacher is the institutional, factory-processing model that we are often locked into. Students, sometimes more than one hundred of them, come and go from our rooms each day. Often, I am so focused on what we are doing, how we are doing it, and what comes next that I don't take the time to find out about my kids' lives outside the classroom. And, after eight years of public schooling, kids get a sense that their lives outside the school really aren't all that relevant anyway. The following is an example of "truth-telling" from Guntown, an example of kids taking over and talking about what matters; it is writing that informs the reader about what it is like to live in this world. This isn't just another writing assignment; this student has something important to say, and she is striving to say it clearly and honestly.

The question is this. Why do you believe that Anne is closer to Pim rather than her mother? My belief is that Anne's views on life are very much like her father's. Mrs. Frank is quite a perfectionist in my way of thinking. Anne cannot and will not even make an attempt to try to behave the way her mother would like her to. She finds her a boring and dull character. If you are to enjoy life, you should definitely have a sense of humor. Anne cannot begin to imagine sitting on the sofa, still, knitting away. She would much rather be outside in her own world, lazily picking a bouquet of flowers and breathing in their fresh sweet beauty. Mrs. Frank is incapable of feeling the same feelings that Anne possesses. It is quite obvious that Mrs. Frank favors Margot and is continuously complaining that Anne doesn't act like a young lady like her sister. "Margot, Margot, Margot!" Anne cries out angrily in one of the scenes of the play. This young girl is caught in a web of silences and fear from which she cannot escape. She is a child longing to feel the sunshine, eat ice cream again, and smell the cool morning air. Her father worries about Anne much more than Margot and I believe that Anne should be worried about more than her tame sister. *She is like a wild horse that even the best cowboys could not defeat.* No one knows what Anne is thinking except her best friend Kitty.

Shanna Duggar, Guntown, Mississippi

Although I don't know Shanna, I have a sense that she would be a good writer, regardless of what happens in school. Phrases like "caught in a web of silences and fear from which she cannot escape" and metaphors like "a wild horse that even the best cowboys could not defeat" indicate a talent and a very bright mind that even public schools as we know them could not squelch. But Shanna wouldn't be able to visit my room without telecommunications. When I put Shanna's work on the overhead projector, the kids look up and read carefully; when they next sit down to write they will have another model, another template of quality writing to draw from, whether they are conscious of it or not.

> My mom's dad served in WWII, but he does not want to talk about it because he had to go around and pick up all the dead bodies. He still has bad dreams about it. He will sometimes talk abut it with his brothers about how he would spend days just picking up parts of people that had been blown up. He always starts to cry when he talks about it.
>
> Bobby Mathews, Guntown, Mississippi

> . . . Based on my experience most people have a good heart. I remember when I went to Oregon this summer. I met this guy at a prison. He got in there by slugging his son. While on the tour of the prison I went to talk with this guy in a little room. I wanted to ask him some questions. I asked him why he abused his son. He told me because he was drunk and he was out of control. But my point is that when the guy was sober, him and his son got along. See, he meant well, but when he was drunk he beat his son. But see, he was good at heart.
>
> Brad Bird, Nikiski, Alaska

> What Anne wrote about people being good at heart may be what she feels is true, but I feel it's false. I mean look at Hitler. Not once did he feel any guilt for what he was doing. He just did what he thought about. He just did what he thought up because HE thought it up.
>
> I can kind of see why Anne said that (good at heart). She had so many people around her who were very kind to her, like Miep and Mr. Kraler. they both put their lives on the line for the Jews. *If all people are good at heart, some just have a teaspoon of goodness.* The way I feel is that everyone is different.
>
> Kate Jones, Corinth, Vermont

> I crouch in the corner of a dark room.
> Will they come for me soon?
> I feel the cold floor on my skin.

And shivers seize my body. I moan from my hunger pains,
wondering why God allows us to wallow in their shame?
I let a sob escape from my scabbed mouth
As I watch them make a grab for my only sister.
I reach out to kiss her . . .
She is gone. I will never see her again.
I listen carefully and I hear the groan of a small child
As a bullet pierces through her flesh.
her body hits the ground.
I hear its mighty sound . . .
I hear the boots of the men
Slushing in the thick mud.
I begin to cry.
I am having trouble breathing now.
I guess this means goodbye.

> Shanna Duggar, Guntown, Mississippi

This past year I had a few students who made inappropriate jokes about the diary and the Holocaust as we were discussing the book. I spoke with them privately about it and didn't get anywhere. In order to figure out what was happening, and in an attempt to stop the distraction, I called the parents of one of the boys. The boy's mother told me that she had had a long talk with her son a few days earlier about the Holocaust, and that it simply terrified him. The boy's parents had rented "Schindler's List" to watch the previous weekend, at his request. But he didn't watch more than thirty minutes of the movie before he left the room, visibly upset. She said that he had also had nightmares after we had watched a video in class with some disturbing pictures from a concentration camp. It was becoming clear to me what was happening. The mother continued to say that she felt her son was simply not mature enough for this material, that he couldn't deal with it emotionally, and that the inappropriate jokes were an effort to avoid the topic. She told me that she would talk with her son and ask him not to disturb the class further; she also reminded me that many eighth-grade students are still children and that a topic like this is going to be very difficult for some of them. Lesson learned. Shanna's poem, vividly describing Anne's death and ending with "I am having trouble breathing now. I guess this means goodbye," speaks for the effect on readers that many students experienced. I struggle with the dark view of humanity that is presented in this book, and its effect on my students, during an often dark and difficult time in their lives. But I reconcile this concern with the realization that part of growing up is recognizing humanity's capability for evil and destruction.

The responses by Bobby, Brad, Kate, and Shanna in the preceding section were from the first year of the conference. In order to suggest that this project wasn't just a flash in the pan, or the kind of project in which everyone works hard to create a one-time spectacle, I'd like to share a few examples of striving writing from the second year of the conference also, and to suggest why I would place each piece in this category. The first response was generated from a prompt by Peggy Turner that articulates one of our greatest concerns as teachers.

> As I was reading a journal last week, I came upon these words that stunned and saddened me. "What's the use of looking forward to the weekend when it's over so fast it seems like it's one minute you're back into hell." Wow! What is it about school that causes a person to write that?
>
> We have read several books this year and have identified and discussed some of the statements made about school and learning in these works. In *To Kill a Mockingbird*, Scout hates school because her teacher restricts Scout's learning sessions with Atticus, her father. "As I inched sluggishly along the treadmill of the Maycomb County school system, I could not help receiving the impression that I was being cheated out of something. Out of what I knew not, yet I did not believe that twelve years of unrelieved boredom was exactly what the state had in mind for me (36)." In Roll of Thunder, Hear My Cry, the teacher gives a great little first-day-of-the-year speech that goes: "(as you are) starting on the road to knowledge and education, may your tiny feet find the pathways of learning steady and forever before you." But Cassie's reaction follows: "Already bored, I stretched my right arm on the desk and rested my head in my upraised hand (19)."
>
> In contrast, Anne is a bright, enthusiastic, albeit talkative, young student who states, "I don't want to be a bad pupil: I should really have stayed in the seventh form in the Montessori school, but was accepted for the Jewish Secondary. When all the Jewish children had to go to Jewish schools, the headmaster took Lies and me conditionally after a bit persuasion. He relied on us to do our best and I don't want to let him down." Anne works very hard not to let him down, but even in hiding is driven to keep up with her work. Anne is a thinker, a reader, and a writer—a lifelong learner and student, inwardly motivated to struggle through the difficult spots. Are you that kind of student? Why or why not? What does your school do well to ensure that you reach your potential? How could it improve so you could learn better? What more could you do?
>
> We look forward to hearing from you soon. It's seventy degrees here in Mississippi and the daffodils are blooming everywhere. Your friend,
>
>   Mrs. T.

Not only has Peggy Turner modeled the practice of good, thoughtful writing, using texts and evidence for her argument (or query in this case), she is addressing the critical issue of personal responsibility, something that Anne will refer to in a later chapter as "self-consciousness." It was simply delightful over the two years we worked together in the conference to receive letters like this from Peggy. Her writing and work online always suggested a certain worldly perspective, a reflective, almost meditative tone, as she considered the diary, her students, and the experience of the conference. Her patient, thoughtful manner was evident in her students' work as well. The online personality of the students from Guntown was perceptive, playful, and at times articulate and creative. Just as the images of sunshine and daffodils brought much-needed color to the darkness of Alaska in February, Peggy's presence online was a key to the success of the conference. I don't think Peggy would mind if I suggested that her writing, both to me personally and to the students in the conference, often had a certain mothering quality, a reassuring, caring, "let me take your hand and show you the way" voice. In looking at the responses that were generated from Peggy's prompt, I found that there were as many students who were upset by the notion of school as hell as there were teachers. In the next response, I think Kylie strives to dispel that notion and does an effective job.

> I think that I'm a good thinker like Anne. I don't understand why people talk so lowly of school . . . I think that deep down somewhere everyone wants to learn. Teachers know how to make learning so fun sometimes. I wish people wouldn't take things for granted so much. We are lucky children. We are lucky we can even go to school. Besides, doesn't our school name mean "where the flounders gather." In Indian (Tlingiit beliefs) flounders were children of fish, so it practically means where the children gather, and isn't that what happens when we go to school: We gather to learn. I feel very sorry for people like that who sit around and mope. Go out and conquer. Make it fun.
>
> Kylie Manning, Juneau, Alaska

Of course teachers like to read words such as Kylie's, in which students articulate good reasons for being in school. But it is more important to realize that the comment from Peggy Turner struck a chord with this student. Kylie has not only disagreed with the statement, she has clearly explained why she feels this way. She is also directly addressing her audience with a clear and distinctive voice. The varied sentence structure also creates a nice rhythm to the piece. When you think about school as a gathering of children, or flounders, it effectively disarms the hell analogy.

One of the traits sometimes exhibited in the striving writing is experimenting with language. During the second year of the conference, Mary Burnham's class wrote poetry as a culminating writing activity. Here are two poems that seem to resonate with the ambience of the experience.

I hear

I hear them coming
and I want to start running.
I hear their guns
I wish I could run.
I hear mothers crying
while children are dying
I hear the world stopping
and everyone watching
I hear my people crying
as they are vainly dying
I hear nothing . . .
There is nothing left to hear.

    Kellie Thomson, Corinth, Vermont

I See Through Windows

I see through windows things
I cannot do
Cannot feel
Cannot breathe.
I see through windows happy families
Happy
Happy
Happy
I am not.
I see through windows
Streets
Shops
Cars
That I cannot
Walk on
Cannot enter
Cannot ride.
I see through windows
Fear
Terror
Hell
I see through windows
Death
Decay
Shadows

    Joshua Leno, Corinth, Vermont

The title of this book is *Exchanging Lives*. Throughout the three years of conference writing that provided the basis for this book, there have been glimpses of life in Mississippi, Vermont, Alaska, and New Mexico, as well as glimpses of divorce, separation from loved ones, life in school, life in the outdoors, and so on. Taken as a whole, the exchanges have allowed students to present themselves to their peers in new ways, to construct their personal "selves" and their communities. Although there have been many pieces of these selves present in the writing, there would be an occasional passage that evoked almost a full sense of the writer. As you read this piece, imagine the young woman carrying a knife and billfold.

> Yes, I do experience sexism around the school, but not in my community. At school I do not fit in with other girls cause they are so refined. I guess that is the word you call it. They look at me as if I have no mind because I am a tomboy. They don't think a girl should hunt and fish or anything guys do. But in my community the guys think it's cool for me to be different. They like me for who I am and the way I am. They tell me that they think there is nothing wrong with wearing boots and carrying a knife and billfold. At least you don't take the chance of leaving your purse somewhere. But, I think the reason I fit in my community is because is because we all were raised together and they know how I was raised as my dad's son, not his daughter. They have seen the way he treats me and all of our hard times we have on the farm. The people you are raised with accept you for who your are, and new people you meet over the years don't always accept you for who you are, instead they think you should be more like them.
>
> Joyce Brown, Guntown, Mississippi

I think we'd all like to have this bright, articulate, independent and insightful student in our classes. Through telecommunications we can come close; we can at least bring her words to our students so that we can broaden our view of the world and ourselves. In this conference, and through the experience of writing about literature online, students can take a stand about who they are and their relationship to the world. And, thankfully, Joyce Brown can "visit" Nikiski and make a statement about standing tall and becoming the person she wants to be.

In my classroom, I sometimes put a large piece of butcher paper on the wall to record the "Golden Lines" pulled from the student writing. If I were to do so with some of the samples we've already looked at in earlier sections, these lines would be on the wall.

I would visit most of my friends and go out in the woods in a space I cleared out 'specially for just lingering. It's by a stream and the sound of the calm water trickling soothes my brain, leaving it open for more thoughts to get in.

I would feel like a caterpillar trapped inside of a tightly closed jelly jar.

Her red hair, slightly parted in the middle, with her warm melting smile would be able to make anyone wake cheerfully.

It seems that she gets to know her dad and herself better, reality, I guess, became more real to her.

If all people are good at heart, some just have a teaspoon of goodness.

She is like a wild horse that even the best cowboys could not defeat.

6 Jenny's Story

Jenny Anderson was a pleasant, productive eighth-grade student in my classroom at Nikiski Middle School two years ago. She read regularly outside the school day, turned in her response notebook, participated in group activities, and was generally conscientious about her work. But social concerns were often foremost in Jenny's mind, as they are for many adolescents. Jenny was a bright, mostly happy, gregarious eighth grader. It was not unusual to see her spend part of her class time reading or writing notes to other students, or pulling another student aside for a clandestine planning session at the back of the room as they entered for class. Although Jenny's grades were above average, I think she would agree that during the first semester there wasn't a high level of personal involvement or risk taking in her school work, particularly in her writing. In this chapter, I'd like to focus on Jenny's writing experiences in my class as they reflect my theory of writing development.

One of the paramount difficulties in the teaching of writing is attributing cause and effect. If we notice a change in a student's writing and ask ourselves why it may have occurred, there are countless variables to consider. Is it a developmental step forward, in which the student's thinking and maturity level has eclipsed a previous level of proficiency? Has the student incorporated a specific concept or technique from a peer response group, or a modeling exercise, or a work of literature that we've been reading? Is the use of metaphor, analogy, or a new form of organization merely experimentation, a haphazard attempt to do something different? Or is it a deliberate attempt to write more effectively? Several curriculum development projects in which I've been involved always seem to result in skills checklists that use descriptors such as "not present," "present," and "proficient" for various writing skills (like using capitalization correctly), suggesting a linear development in these areas. Without launching into a major theoretical discussion of curriculum and assessment, I'd like next to put forth my theory of writing development.

The "A Day in the Life" piece in Chapter 1 provided a view of this theory in action. I'm sure you'll recognize the work of Donald Graves, Nancie Atwell, and the Goodmans in my pedagogy. Before we look at Jenny's year in my classroom, I think it's important to state the four pillars of my beliefs as clearly and concisely as possible. First and foremost, language development varies widely from one child to the next. In a teacher-research project last year, I conducted in-depth interviews of six students to learn their processes for writing and revising poetry. I was shocked to learn how little I knew about these students and their writing processes; furthermore, I knew little about the differences between the individual students in terms of their gathering of ideas, processing language, finding response to their work, the how, what, and where of the editing process, and so on. A recent survey of my homeroom class revealed that only two of the twenty-four students had eaten even vaguely similar breakfasts in the morning. If students don't approach the first meal in the morning with any sense of uniform process, content, or intent, how can we assume that something as complex as writing will be similar among them? Second, immersion in real language activities is the single most important factor in language development; in real language activities kids listen, speak, and write in meaningful exchanges, making real choices in terms of how they engage in these activities. Third, there is a place for direct, explicit instruction from teacher to student in all language areas. Last, in order for a student to grow as a reader, writer, speaker, and listener, there must be a positive, nurturing environment; at its core is the student's relationship with the teacher, who must consistently model the attributes of a proficient language user and demonstrate the principle of learning through observation.

To be honest, Jenny's development as a writer didn't get my attention until I read a very good piece of writing that she was planning to send to another class in the exchange. I had met with her about her poetry and her oral history earlier in the year. I had read and responded to her response journal throughout the first semester. But it wasn't until I was pleasantly surprised by what was obviously a major leap for her as a writer that I looked closely at her experience. All teachers, particularly writing teachers, have students they are drawn to. For me, it is the hardworking, creative, divergent thinkers: kids whose writing makes an impression and stands out from others' in the pile of paper. I feel somewhat guilty about the fact that I don't spend nearly as much time and energy with the reluctant or lazy writers as I used to. I find myself leaning toward the stronger writers more and more as I gain experience in working with these motivated writers. So, although I certainly had provided Jenny with an opportunity for success, and quality response, I had not given her the same attention as I had to some other writers in my classes. Frankly, although Jenny made considerable progress as a writer, eventually earning my Writer of the

Year award, there were more effective writers in that eighth-grade class: kids who had entered the year as writers with a distinctive voice, a stronger vocabulary, more tools in their bag of tricks, and who wrote better poems and essays. Yet I've selected Jenny's story to tell because I think it presents an opportunity to actually see and discuss the causes and effects of her growth as a writer.

I'd like to look closely at several of Jenny's writing experiences over the course of one school year in my classroom, and reflect and speculate on what I can learn as a teacher from this sequence. I've chosen four activities to discuss: Jenny's first writing (poetry) of the school year, her experience as part of the Anne Frank Conference, her revision of one of her responses into an essay, and her analytic writing assessment piece. Writing through telecommunications was not a magic catalyst that propelled Jenny into a new realm of efficacy in writing, but it clearly helped prepare her to enter high school as a much better writer than she had been the previous August. This was a pivotal time for her.

In early October, as part of our interdisciplinary study of Nikiski, I took my students to Bishop Creek, an event described in detail in my "A Day in the Life" piece. This is one of my favorite days of the school year, not only as a teacher but as a writer. Earlier, we looked at Jessica's poem, "The Stirring," which I still consider to be one of the best pieces of student writing that I have ever read. But that piece was an exception. A lot of good writing happens out at Bishop Creek; there, kids use the natural environment as a pool of observations to bring their writing to life, to illustrate their ideas and emotions. However, there is also a lot of writing that shows that this kind of "connecting" just doesn't happen for some kids, as I think Jenny's poem exemplifies. The following is her final draft, after five revisions of the original poem.

Untitled

Bigger fish eat little fish,
Someone once said,
And they come from beyond the dark blue waters,
They swim with such grace,
And with such ease,
That it makes you wonder,
Why do we harm such beautiful creatures.
To swim as a fish,
Would be something great and new,
I am sure,
That if you thought about it,
you would want to.

I know that life,
will never be like Gone with the Wind,
But a tiny harmless creature,
swimming through the rolling waves,
doesn't need ourselves killing them off.

Jennifer Anderson

What has happened with this piece of writing? After looking through the various drafts, I sensed that Jenny began with a question that came to her while she was on the beach at Bishop Creek: why do humans kill innocent creatures? Her poem, then, is an attempt to answer this question, and to look at the question from the perspective of fish. Jenny has used some sensory description to bring the piece alive: the dark blue waters, the rolling waves, swimming with grace, and so on. These are scenes we can envision as we read. Jenny has found an interesting idea to write about. Unfortunately for me as a reader, the piece falls short of accomplishing the idea because of the clichés ("bigger fish eat little fish" and "life will never be like Gone with the Wind"), the lack of flow and rhythm in the poem, the awkward constructions (as in the last line), and, above all, the lack of voice. If you were to talk to Jenny about her experience at Bishop Creek (or about the basketball game on Friday night, or about her favorite movie), the person's voice you would hear would be very different from the voice of the person "telling" this poem.

I am convinced that one of my missions as a writing teacher is to lead students, through a wide variety of language experiences, to find their voices. Over the course of an entire school year, my students wrote formal and informal responses to literature, extensive oral histories, poetry based on a sense of place, collaborative short plays, personal essays, and regular reflective writings about themselves as learners. For some students, their voices came through right away in their poetry. Others found their voices in oral histories, and others in personal essays. Some students only loosened up and let their real voices be heard in the response journals that I alone would read. And many students discovered their voices in the Anne Frank Conference.

In all these literary pursuits, I think the key factor was *connectedness* with the audience. For some kids, the idea of having their poetry and oral histories published in a school anthology created the idea of an authentic audience for them; for others it was the audience who would see their plays, or the knowledge that their personal essays would be shared with the class. For Jenny, as best as I can tell, it was the opportunity to write to other students within the Anne Frank Conference that inspired her to release the genuine voice that previously had been reserved for notes to friends and talk in the school hallways.

In order to talk about connectedness, and to refer again to the type of writing I call "connecting writing," I'd like to share a sequence of events involving Jenny and the Anne Frank Conference. I wouldn't say that this is a typical experience for all students, but I would suggest that these types of connections do happen often in a literary exchange, and that there is no other way, at least that I'm aware of, to duplicate the kind of energy and enthusiasm unleashed with this type of connection.

Jenny's story begins during the second week of the 1995 Anne Frank Conference. The following prompt came from Mississippi.

> Our prompt from Sumrall, Mississippi, for week two (Feb. 5):
>
> Anne says, "In spite of everything, I still believe that people are really good at heart."
>
> Do you believe this? What about the Nazis and any people with prejudice and cruelty? Can all people really be good at heart? Why or why not?

Before we responded to the prompt, I shared with the students the responses to our prompt during the first week. We were particularly impressed with the thoughtful responses from Phil Sittnick's class in Laguna, New Mexico. We talked about why these responses were effective, and we brainstormed some ideas for our responses. I told the students that their typed responses could be included in their response notebooks for credit. (My students are very grade motivated: without points attached, I seldom see kids motivated by an intrinsic desire to learn.) Since I now have ten computers in the room, I divided the class in half, and each group was granted one full period on the computer. The plan was for each student to write a response, print it out, and confer with another student about the response before sending it off. Since the responses tended to be about two paragraphs in length, this seemed doable. Jenny was in the first group. At the end of the period the students saved their work. When we went to switch groups the next day, Jenny and a few other students asked if they could have more time to write their responses. I said that they could; since there were several absences that day, there were a few extra computers available. The following morning, before school, I gathered all the responses from both days into two large files to proofread and send to BreadNet. As I was proofreading, I saw the usual range of quality and investment. Some students had obviously used the time to its fullest and had carefully considered the prompt in the light of the text. Others had merely gone through the motions to get the assignment done. As a whole, though, I was pleased with the results, and considered the batch to be a notch up from the informal responses we often do.

As I read, a few of the writings caught my eye. One of these was Jenny's. It was the first time during the school year that I had heard Jenny's voice, the first time that she had taken a risk and experimented with language. It was immediately clear to me that this was more than an assignment to Jenny. Here is a first draft of her response with only a few minor proofreading changes. Later in the quarter Jenny would use the following response as the basis for a formal personal essay.

> My name is Jennifer Anderson. I am 13 and go to Nikiski Middle School. Personally, I think that everyone is born with a good or bad heart. But, that doesn't mean that people born with bad hearts, grow up to be bad at heart. I believe everyone has the chance to become whatever they want to be. So, even people born right, can turn sour at any time and moment. But, even with all the problems surrounding us, most people, do really become good at heart. So in some ways, Anne Frank is right. But, it's not just some gift from God, even though he can help you. It comes right down to who you want to be and what you feel you need to be.
>
> I think the Nazis, deep down inside, have turned sour, but that doesn't mean that they can't turn over a new leaf at any time. Sometimes, people have to be the wind to make people like the Nazis turn over their leaf and start again. So even if they are not good at heart now, it doesn't mean they don't have any more chances to become a good and loving person. They are just like everyone else, but turned bad. I believe everyone has to work at becoming a good person, even if they were born that way. Anne says "Then I fall asleep with a stupid feeling of wishing to be different from what I am or from what I want to be." At the beginning of the book, I wasn't too impressed by Anne. But now it seems that she's changing her personality and becoming a better person. Not that she was a bad person to begin with, but maybe in this case, the Nazis were the wind and they blew Anne to the point of growing up and turning over her leaf.
>
> Jen Anderson, Nikiski, Alaska

What is remarkable to me about this piece is Jenny's first attempt to use a metaphor in her writing. The idea of Anne Frank as a leaf, caught in the winds of the Holocaust, is a powerful, effective image. Not only has Jenny thought seriously about the question asked by the students at Sumrall, she has been purposeful in her attempt to express her ideas in a clear and interesting manner. Jenny's response most clearly represents the traits that I describe in discussing "connecting writing." Here, there seems to be little doubt that the writer has connected with the reader and that the writing is purposeful in some way.

In looking at the transcript from the first year of the conference and reading it several times for a variety of purposes, there were times when I had difficulty differentiating between "reaching" and "connecting" writing. However, it is clear that both categories exist; for that reason I tried to select samples that clearly fell into one group or the other. Regardless of the category for the preceding piece of writing by Jenny, I can see a voice emerging in that work. Phrases such as "I am . . . , I think . . . , I believe . . . ," and "it's not just some gift from God . . ." are very different from the clichéd, clumsy constructions of her earlier work. Neither her poetry nor her journal responses reflected the kind of energy, thought, and commitment that is clearly present in this piece. This is how Jenny would speak in a discussion; her writing is free of the pseudo-formal, please-the-teacher kind of language that so often permeates students' responses to literature at this age. As Jenny later explained in her reflective writing, that earlier work was an attempt to "finish the assignment like any other schoolwork."

We had discussed the effective use of metaphor in class. Impressively, and without any nudge from me, Jenny attempts to illustrate her idea through a quote from the text. It is these small victories, when students clearly step forward into a new realm as writers, that keep me excited about education. This was a big day for Jenny. Whether she realized it or not, she was becoming a better writer. To celebrate and to model good writing and risk taking, I shared Jenny's piece with all my classes. Jenny was not used to this kind of attention—being portrayed as a writer and a creative, thoughtful student in front of her classmates. She was somewhat embarrassed, but clearly pleased.

These exchanges do not always hum along like clockwork. During the year Jenny participated, the Anne Frank Conference stalled for a while, due to several snags that occurred during the second week. One teacher had not received her book order, another had to take a family-illness leave from school, and one class was having trouble getting access to computers. Another teacher was having trouble posting the writing in the conferences because he was telnetting to BreadNet, an added difficulty. This, as you know, is the reality of school. The best-laid plans do not always come to fruition, but we do learn that perseverance pays off. As the coordinator of the conference, I, too, was at fault. After having worked with the same group of teachers for two years, I don't think I explained the process that third conference year as clearly as I could have. Unfortunately, Jenny's piece, together with all our responses from that week, went unanswered. Finally, after some discussion by the teachers in the conference, we regrouped and the conference took off again during the third week. It was then, after Jenny's second posting, that she discovered the power of connectedness. It began with a prompt from Laguna.

> From: Philip Sittnick
> Subject: Laguna's Prompts
> To: Third
>
> Hey Y'all:
>
> We're having a blast telecommunicating with everyone out there—it's more fun than a barrel of monkeys, or even reading about a girl and her family hiding out in a dinky apartment. No, seriously, we are enjoying the exchange, and have put together some prompts that we'd like you to respond to when you catch your breath and get a chance.
>
> Saturday, 7 November, 1942
> "I have in my mind's eye an image of what a perfect mother and wife should be; and in whom I must call 'Mother' I find no trace of that image."
>
> What is your image of the "perfect Mother"? Does your own Mother live up to your imagined ideal Mom? Why or why not?
>
> > 8th grade students at Laguna Middle School
> >
> > > "Where Eagles Soar"

Jenny selected the question about the "perfect mother" and responded:

> HAPPY VALENTINE'S DAY! My name's Jenny and I just thought I'd drop you a line and answer a few questions that you have. So howdy, and away we go. My mother is nowhere near being the perfect mother, even though she tries. I think being the perfect mother has to do with friendship and commitment to one another. Not that every mother isn't committed, but a different kind of commitment. Like the secrets you make at midnight with your best friend when she finally finds out who you like, or when you find out that there is a nasty rumor going around school about you, and you and your best friend go beat up whoever started it. (HA!) I might know one person with a somewhat near okay mother, but she doesn't appreciate her. Now don't get any crazy ideas like I don't love my mom. I do, it's just that sometimes (every mom does this) she tries a little too hard. Well, it's been real, but times runnin' out.
>
> BYEBYEBYEBYEBYE

Obviously, this is a much different kind of writing than Jenny's first response. It is much more like a note that she might pass, more informal, less "literary." The writing has a lively voice; I like the line about "secrets you make at midnight." Here, Jenny is talking in frank terms about her life and what she values. My thirteen-year-old niece has lived with us for a couple of years. I've seen firsthand the deadly seriousness and profound solemnity that surround these "secrets you make at midnight." There is also a playful tone in Jenny's writing that makes this note come alive. Jenny wrote this response on Valentine's Day, by far the most significant of all holidays in the middle school, a day in which academic concerns generally rank close to the observation of wallpaper patterns and political trends in the Middle East in my students' realm of thinking. (One tiny mass-produced Ziggy valentine from the right boy or girl can render the entire universe irrelevant until the adolescent body and mind has had sufficient pause to process the uncomfortable surge in hormonal disturbance.) Despite the holiday and the logistical problems with the conference, we managed to get a new plan going, reaffirming our commitment to making it work; the conference was again alive. The writing began to flow through the wires.

Less than a week after posting our responses, a file arrived from Phil Sittnick's class in Laguna; there were eleven responses addressed to Jenny. There were three responses from Sumrall, all addressed to Jenny. Most students received one or two responses. Another student had five direct replies. A few students received no response. As soon as Jenny's responses arrived, I printed them out and gave them to her. Her face lit up and she bounced out of her seat, exclaiming, "They wrote back to *ME?* What did they say? Let me see!" As I handed her the folder, I realized that she had never read anything in my class with this sort of intensity before, except for the intricately folded personal notes from other students. It dawned on me, again, that this is why these literary exchanges generate such enthusiasm. The students *connect* with other students. I, the teacher, am merely the facilitator, the conduit for passing the writing back and forth through the technology. Here are a few of the responses from Laguna.

> Dear Jenny,
>
> Hello there! My name is Mary Chavez. I am 14 years old and very short for my age. Well, I just thought I would write to you. So you don't think your mom is a perfect mother huh? Well, my mom is almost perfect but sometimes she can also try too hard too. I can tell my mom almost anything but there are some

things that I don't tell her because she would probably ground me or something like that. I think what you're saying about best friends is true!

But you have to make sure you can trust them, but with mothers you already have their trust because you have known them all your life! That is a real important thing about different relationships with peers (don't you think?). I love my mom too but sometimes I don't act like it because I either talk back to her or we get in a argument and I tell her that I don't really love her but deep down inside I do really love her. Well I guess I'll end here so I could write to some other people. Later.

Mary Chavez, Laguna, New Mexico

Dear Jenny,

Hello. My name is Monica Waikaniwa. I just thought that I would respond to you about your paragraph. So, lets get with it. I agree with you about what you wrote, when you were talking about the perfect mother. I know that my mom doesn't come close to being the perfect mother. But, at least she tries to do her best. I love my mom.

Monica Waikaniwa, Laguna, New Mexico

Dear Jenny Anderson,

Happy Valentine's Day to you, too (even a little late). My name is Nicole Arkie. I just thought I would type back to you. Before I tell anyone my secrets I have to see how they are so I can tell them what I've got to say. My mom don't live with me— we're separated. I don't know why I'm telling you this because I don't even know you, but you seem to be nice understanding person. Well that's all that I can think of right now so bye!

Sincerely,
Nicole Arkie, Laguna, New Mexico

Dear Jenny Anderson,

Hello There! My name is Robyn Leon. I'm an eighth grader at Laguna Middle School. I thought your response was cool. Why aren't you and your mother like that? For my mother and me, we're kind of like that. I mean we can talk openly but sometimes she always has too much to say about what I tell her. That's the only thing I don't like about her plus a lot more, but I'd rather not say. Not like I don't like her it's just that she does things to bug me and she knows just how to get me mad. I know what you mean when you say some mothers try too hard. Sometimes I think my mother tries too hard too. That's all I have to say about your response. So until then, Later.

Only Me, Robyn Leon, Laguna, New Mexico

Dear Jenny Anderson,

Well, hello, I'm Terri and I thought I would write back to you. Well, I want to know how does your mom try too hard to be the perfect mother? Why do you think that the perfect mother has to have friendship and commitment to each other? Well, I have a really close perfect mother. Even though she's not around that much, she tries to see me as often as she can. Because my parents are divorced but she lives like 3-4 miles away. Well, in my mother she can keep all the secrets I tell her. Mostly when they're stuff that I can't tell my dad, so she's very close to the perfect mother. So you can see I do love my mother a lot.

Well, Bye for now!!!!!
A Friend,
Terri Jose, Laguna, New Mexico

Dear Jenny Anderson,

Hello, my name is Cara Francisco. I just thought that I would respond back to you about my mother. My mother is the perfect mom for me because I think she is an expert at taking care of me and my family. You would have thought she was an expert with all of my brothers and sisters—there are 8 of us, and you can always count on her and you know that she will always be there for me and the rest of my family if we had a problem. So I think that my mom is the perfect mom for me. Well, sorry I didn't write much.

Sincerely,
Cara Francisco, Laguna, New Mexico

Imagine coming to class as an eighth grader and discovering messages from students across the country, responding to something you have written. Jenny was thrilled as she shared the replies with other students. Some of them were disappointed that they had not received responses to their writing, an unfortunate reality within these exchanges. There is no way to arrange it so that all students are guaranteed responses to their writing. It was, however, a big moment for Jenny. She and another student who also had received multiple replies volunteered to stay in the classroom to work on their replies while the rest of the eighth-grade class was taking part in our school's snow sculpture contest. Here is Jenny's response to Cara:

Dear Cara Francisco,

I think that's great that you have a perfect relationship with your mother. I wish I did, but our relationship could use a lot of work. Maybe, you could send me some pointers on how to make my mother and mine relationship better. I know what makes a good relationship, I just can't seem to be able to apply it to my own life. What's it like to have eight kids in your family? There are five kids in mine. It's hard to have a voice in a big family, but I try to get my point across. Is it like that in your family? Thanks for writing to me. Bye!

Sincerely,
Jenny Anderson, Nikiski, Alaska

Although the preceding exchange between Jenny and the students at Laguna has elements of several of the categories I've described, I think it is most clearly an example of connecting writing. Simply put, the writing attempts to connect ideas from the text and the prompts to the writers' lives and personal experiences, with a specific audience in mind. The students were talking about such real issues as motherhood, separation, and getting along with family members in a direct and purposeful way. None of the messages above began with trite "writing starters" like "I love my mother because. . . ." This writing was spontaneously generated by the students. It was through this kind of writing that Jenny discovered the immediacy and power of writing; in her own words, this writing wasn't just something she did to "finish the assignment like any other schoolwork."

After the conference ended, my students had the opportunity to take one of the responses that they had written as part of the exchange and to expand the piece into a personal essay. Writing personal essays is a difficult task for eighth graders (or for anyone, for that matter). Before entering the eighth grade in our school system, students typically had written only fiction stories, research papers, and an occasional book report. Responses to literature—let alone a structured, logical, organized response—were assignments that were completely foreign, and often intimidating, to my students. But part of my job is to challenge students, to take them and their package of language tools as far as they can go during the year. It is in those personal essays, such as Annabeth's in the introduction to this book, that I often discover some of the best writing of the school year. Of course, that best writing just doesn't happen for some kids. They are too immature, too disorganized, too distracted, or, frankly, too disassociated with the entire school program to invest in a writing project like this. Like Annabeth, Jenny has used Anne Frank's diary to read her own life, and her own life to read the diary; such association is at the heart of understanding literature. In the following essay, which begins with her original response in the conference, Jenny takes the idea a few steps further into what I consider to be an effective piece of writing. Listen to her voice as you read this essay.

Personally, I think that everyone is born with a good or bad heart. But, that does not mean that people born with bad hearts grow up to be bad at heart. I believe that everyone had the chance to become whatever they want to be. So, even people born right, can turn sour at any time. Even with all the problems surrounding us, most people really do become good at heart. So, in some ways, Anne Frank is right. But, it's not just some gift from God, even though he can help you. It comes right down to who you want to be and who you feel you need to be.

I think the Nazis deep down inside turned sour, but it wasn't like they couldn't turn over a new leaf and start again. Sometimes, people need to be the wind to make people like the Nazis turn over their leaf and become a good and loving person. Even if they were having a rough time, it doesn't mean they don't have any more chances to become good at heart. They are just like everyone else, but have turned bad. I believe everyone has to work at becoming a good person, even if they weren't born that way. In Anne's diary, she says, "then I fall asleep with a stupid feeling of wishing to be different then what I am or what I want to be." (Saturday, 28 November 1942) At the beginning of the book, I wasn't too impressed with Anne. But, now it seems that Anne is changing and becoming a better person, not that she was a bad person to begin with. Maybe in this case, the Nazis were the wind and they blew Anne to the point of growing up and turning over her leaf.

When I was younger, I believed that I would always have a good heart, and so would everyone else. But, as time went on, I woke up and smelled the coffee. I became more and more involved with myself and my heart was slowly turning sour. I couldn't see it, until I was talking about someone behind their back, and I realized that everything that I said about that person, was just like describing myself. Finally, I decided to make a change about myself. In my case I used myself as the wind to turn over my leaf.

I think sometimes, we all have our bad days. But, we shouldn't let unhappiness take us over, when we do that we are giving in to all the Nazis of the world. Take a lesson from Anne Frank. She did everything she could to stay cheerful, and keep the family together. There are thin strings that hold a family together. Even though the Frank family's string broke, Anne Frank still has her strings tied to her diary, and in some ways, holds my life, and every other person who has had the privilege of reading this book. So if you have the choice, stay happy, because maybe someday you'll end up like Anne Frank. She left behind a memory of happiness and goodness. If what happened to her happened you, what would people remember about you?

Let me reemphasize what a difficult task a personal essay like this is for eighth graders. Typically, students write one opinion after another, without developing the ideas or using the text—let alone metaphors or personal experience—to illustrate their ideas. Then, through response, conferencing, drafting, and revision, the piece gradually becomes (or doesn't become) a singular piece. Jenny's piece contains the main elements that I was looking for in this assignment, elements that I explained and wrote on a class assignment sheet at the start of the process. Jenny has stated an opinion—that people are basically good at heart, but can be led astray—and she has supported this opinion through the text and her own experience. In short, Jenny has met the terms of the assignment in a clear and convincing way. Even more rewarding to me is that I see a confident, purposeful, risk-taking writer here. Jenny has again experimented with metaphor, with the string that binds families together. Although it is somewhat clichéd, the "wake up and smell the coffee" phrase is lively and playful. If we look at the piece as a whole, I see what I long for most in student writing, a student making sense of her life and her world through the close reading of literature and the writing about it. I teach eighth grade because kids are still making these important discoveries: that, yes, sometimes *they* are the ones talking behind someone's back (perhaps even *about* someone talking behind someone's back); that life isn't always the joyous, carefree experience that we had as children (or the time we choose to remember as childhood); and so on. Frankly, Jenny's last question, "If what happened to her happened to you, what would people remember about you?" is a profound and troubling notion for most adolescents, or even for most people. An eighth grader's typical reply might be something like this: "Well . . . that depends. If I were remembered for my life up until two weeks ago, it wouldn't be too good, but now that I have everything figured out and I made the basketball team . . . it would be okay." Perhaps I'm trivializing an important issue here, but my point is that through literature and writing, and also through exchanges in which kids' troubling questions and speculations about human nature are heard and considered, kids grow . . . as writers, as readers, and as people.

Each spring our district conducts an analytic writing assessment for all students in grades 4, 6, 8, and 10. Each student in these grades receives a sheet of several prompts to choose from as a basis for writing. Students are then given three class periods to write, revise, and edit their work. The system is flawed in important ways. First of all, the prompts elicit widely varying genres from the students, from fiction to letters to the editor. Since the evaluation rubric remains the same, the results of an evaluation of a heartfelt personal essay logically cannot be compared to an evaluation of a letter to the editor. Further, students are not allowed to bring the writing out of the classroom during the three days of the assessment, nor are they allowed to ask for response to their writing. In classrooms where students typically have had time to write, and have been encouraged to write in an environment that is most conducive to their writing, as well as to continually seek response, these writing assessment conditions are stifling. Ostensibly, the purpose of these assessment rules (like the rule that all writers must use black pens) is to create uniform writing conditions for all the students. Although not explicitly stated, the district's goal is to enable the comparison of writing programs from one school to another, not to provide diagnostic evaluations of writing for students and teachers. That said, this assessment still is a huge step forward from the usual norm-referenced standardized tests in which students fill in bubbles within a category such as "written expression" in order to gauge their writing skills. The current assessment evaluates six writing traits, each clearly articulated on a detailed rubric. These trait categories are: Ideas and Content, Organization, Effective Word Choice, Voice/Tone/Flavor, Sentence Structure, and Writing Conventions. Each category receives up to five points, for a maximum possible total of thirty points. Since two readers read each paper, the maximum possible score is sixty points. If the two readers are more than a point apart on any of the traits, a third reader evaluates the writing. Someday I will work in a system that doesn't require numeric value in order to evaluate something.

During the spring when Jenny was in my class, one of the most controversial prompts in the district's writing assessment involved the age-old sports-versus-academics debate, an argument that was also debated vigorously in our community and in our school faculty lounge. The prompt stated that there was public pressure to eliminate sports and extracurricular activities in order to provide more funding for academic programs. Since many of our students come to school mainly for these activities, and rank academics as a distant second in terms of motivators, this prompt elicited many lively responses. Unfortunately, most of the responses were little more than lively. Students often listed a series of opinions about why they liked basketball, or why school would "suck" without sports, and so forth. There were some sophisticated arguments; but, because of the emotions surrounding the issue, most of my students who wrote on this topic did not score well. They lost sight of the analytic traits in their passionate defense of activities.

As I sat down to review the writing and the assessments that were returned, I was very pleased to see that more than 15 of the 78 students who participated had scored higher than 50 points. As a teacher, whether I agree or disagree with the purpose or method of an assessment, I always pray that my kids do well. Two students had scored higher than 55, the cutoff for the exemplar or star papers, which are subsequently published in a districtwide anthology. One of the pieces to score 57 points was Jenny Anderson's. I have to say that I was surprised. I knew Jenny had come a long way this year; but, in the assessment's three years up to that time, and with more than 250 students participating, only five papers had been scored that high. Jenny's piece, given below, is radically different from her Anne Frank essay, but I do think it is a solid piece of writing, resulting from her confidence and newly discovered energy and commitment for writing.

I believe that sports are a positive part of our school district. People love sports and admire the people who play them. It becomes a part of them and if they're taking that away from them, where are they going to go to fill that empty void? Sports boost kids' interests in school, friends, and life. It's time that they're spending positively, instead of getting into trouble.

The fact that there are major arguments going on about this issue is frightening. People say that it takes money and time away from learning. It's true that it does take time and money, but the kids are learning. The coaches teach them about team work, sportsmanship, and hard work. The reason kids need to know this is because learning to work together is an important part of life and teams just help you get a head start.

I have nothing against getting the fullest education possible. But, some kids are not interested in school as much as others. They need a reason for coming to school. If sports is that reason, isn't it worth it?

Sports are wonderful for kids' self-esteem. It teaches them how to be a team player, no matter how good or bad a game you had. It also helps them realize that they are someone and they aren't just a "nobody." As long as there are sports in the school, kids will continue to come to school and feel that there is a purpose for their presence there.

High school sports can also help you get into college. People who could have never afforded to go, now with sports, they have the chance. Sports are helping kids go on to higher education.

Sports teach responsibility and new skills. Kids look up to great athletes as their role models. It's important to have a positive role model, instead of one that can get you into trouble. Sports are something that should be a part of school and should always stay that way.

When I read this piece, I was struck by its systematic organization, the focus of each paragraph, the elaboration on the central ideas in the piece. There is no extra "fluff" in this piece, nothing that should be cut out to tighten the overall argument. I shared Jenny's articulate and reasoned piece with several coaches and teachers in the school, and they encouraged me to ask her to send it to the local newspaper for publication the following fall, when the antifootball chorus would be most vocal.

At the beginning of this chapter, I talked about how difficult it is to attribute cause and effect in teaching writing. Obviously, one of the major contributing factors to Jenny's development as a writer this year is Jenny's development as a human being. Compared to the Jenny who entered my classroom in August, the person who wrote this essay is definitely a more mature and confident young woman. But I do think that there were several additional factors that contributed to her obvious and substantial growth as a writer. First, she was immersed in a wide variety of language experiences throughout the year, in which she made real choices in her learning. Next, she found an authentic audience for her writing, which compelled her to strive for a new efficacy in her writing. There is no doubt that the response to her writing on Anne Frank was a major impetus for her increased confidence and risk taking. Last, she was learning in a positive, nurturing environment, one in which the students (and the teacher) were encouraged to take risks. In this profession it is so easy to focus on the student who has been absent for two weeks, or who has lost his writing portfolio, or who has refused to put her words on paper; but it is absolutely critical that we as teachers take the time to look closely at what goes well and to share these experiences with one another. Out of the eighty-seven students in my classroom, including Jenny, who started high school the next year, there were probably only a handful who reflected back on eighth grade as a year that was a turning point for them in terms of their development as writers. Nevertheless, as a whole they did move forward, and I can take solace in the fact that this kind of growth *could happen* in my classroom.

7 Networking Diversity

Think of wonderful things. Be proud of who you are . . . .
Darne Durden, Guntown, Mississippi

Up to this point we've moved from a discussion of my pedagogy and philosophy of teaching writing to a close look at student writings, including one student's writing experience in particular. In this chapter I'd like to return to a discussion of some of the larger issues and implications of a project like this.

I started teaching in a homogenous classroom of Alaskan Yup'ik students. These early experiences of teaching in another culture, very different from my own, shaped my views of teaching in important ways. I learned that through reading, discussing, and writing about literature with people from another culture, I was forced to question my own perceptions in novel and compelling ways that would otherwise not have occurred. For instance, during my student teaching experience, I had read *Of Mice and Men* with students in a mill town in western Montana. In the American West, where individuality and independence are prized qualities, there wasn't much debate about whether George had done the right thing by ending Lenny's life. The students, for the most part, felt that George should not be burdened by the responsibility of taking care of Lenny, and that the shooting was a reasonable decision. In the isolated Yup'ik community (four hundred miles from the nearest city) where people spend their entire lives in close proximity, the students expressed outrage at George's action. They felt that the problems that Lenny had created were actually George's fault, because George had not taken adequate care to keep Lenny out of trouble. In the Yup'ik community, everyone is responsible for one another—for gathering food, for healing the sick, for raising the children. Putting your own needs above those of your family or those of the community is not acceptable. Through our reading, discussing, and writing about this novel, I learned a great deal about my students and seriously questioned my own reading of the novel, as well as my own perceptions of independence, the pursuit of happiness, and the collective responsibility of an individual in a community. In Nunapitchuk, where Yup'ik is still the first language, the phrase "It takes a village to raise a child" is not a cliché.

After leaving the village, I taught in a multicultural setting in a hub town for many of the Yup'ik villages on the Kuskokwim Delta. There, the ideal discussion for me as a teacher was the kind of discussion which included widely disparate views of a text, as students processed the language through the lens of their different cultures. As we read folktales from around the world, the culture of the text added another dimension of complexity. Simply put, I became dependent on these multiple viewpoints during literary discussions. When I moved to Nikiski, a small town on the Kenai Peninsula with little ethnic diversity, I found myself longing for those rich, complicated discussions. Soon, I was making assumptions about how my students would react to a particular text or event in the classroom. Unfortunately, I think this experience is all too common in our schools; we forget that there are very different lenses for reading literature and thus reading our lives. As Beverly J. Moss and Keith Walters point out in "Rethinking Diversity: Axes of Difference in the Writing Classroom," the notion of differing views is easily submerged by the dominant culture and its perceptions toward literacy.

> At least since earlier this century when large-scale standardized examinations began to play a major role in American education, schools and universities in the country have operated largely as if diversity did not matter. Despite what a great deal of scholarly research has revealed and what our common sense teaches us, we as teachers often continue to evaluate ourselves and our students as if there were a single, appropriate way of using language and of being literate.

Our community has a large number of people who have come from Oklahoma, Texas, Louisiana, and other states with large oil companies to work in the local oil fields. Unfortunately, they've brought many of their prejudices with them to Alaska. Unlike other areas of Alaska, Nikiski has a very small native population. Although we are aware of the presence of racism in our town, it is difficult to deal with in the classroom. Diverse viewpoints from other cultures simply aren't present, or they are so dominated by the majority culture that they aren't heard.

Why teach "diversity?" It seems ludicrous to have to answer this question, but it is a question to which teachers must respond. If celebrating diversity in our classrooms were a priority across the country, perhaps we wouldn't have bigoted legislation like Proposition 103 in California. The answer to a misguided idea such as this one is not to defeat the bill but to defeat the ignorance and prejudice that allowed it to come into existence in the first place. Deborah Meier, in her wonderful book, *The Power of Their Ideas*, makes an eloquent argument for recognizing, honoring, and celebrating diversity in the classroom.

> Public schools can train us for such political conversation across divisions of race, class, religion, and ideology. It is often in the clash of irreconcilable ideas that we can learn how to test or revise ideas, or invent new ones. Both teachers and students need to search for metaphors that work across ideological, historical, and personal differences. We cannot assume everyone will react the same way to the theory of evolution, the "discovery" of America, the Gulf War, or the value of "life-style" choices. Differences make things complicated. (p. 7)

This diversity (rather than passive homogeneity) is difficult to achieve in my classroom. The first exchange that is presented next is an example of a step toward that complexity. This particular exchange, as part of the Anne Frank Conference, was a powerful lesson about how we can bring diversity into a largely homogeneous classroom. This exchange profoundly affected one of my former students, Shauntae Steward. At the time he was in my class, he was one of only two black students in a school of more than five hundred. One of the online discussion classes posted a prompt asking the other students to write about prejudice. Shauntae, a reluctant writer, stayed after the bell to finish his response. With his permission, I typed it for him and sent it directly to Peggy Turner with a short note asking for her students to respond directly to Shauntae's writing; I knew that I could count on Peggy. The very next day, Shauntae received numerous responses—too many to print here. In class, I printed them and copied them onto an overhead transparency. As we read them aloud and discussed them, I realized that it was the first time that we had discussed prejudice seriously, openly, and with minority perspectives as the basis for discussion. Naturally, Shauntae was walking on air when he saw that these students, representatives from an entire class, were writing to him! Here is Shauntae's response, followed by some examples of the responses he received in the exchange.

To Carol Bell, Guntown MS

My name is Shauntae Steward. I am a black male. I am 14. I can kind of understand Anne Frank. For me, being black, I don't know what it is, but people feel they have to be bigger than me. I myself have hidden away from skin heads for more than six hours. I know how scary it is to hear someone coming or talking and thinking if they find you they very well might kill you. I am one of two black kids in a school of over 500. I don't get much trouble at school. Well, I don't know what it is that brings about prejudice, but I wish we could end it.

From,
Shauntae Steward, Nikiski, Alaska

Dear Shantae,

Hi. I'm Mrs. Turner, and I thank you for your wonderful letter. Don't you just love this electronic connection? Mr. C. put your letter online last night at nine, and my first period class in Saltillo, Mississippi, read it on the overhead at 8:00 this morning. I am sitting here at nine o'clock after a long rainy day at school with about seventy letters in my lap addressed to you, so we will see how many I can get on before I fall on the floor.

Mrs. T. (Peggy Turner), Guntown, Mississippi

Dear Shauntae,

I'm now responding back to your letter; I've never been in trouble with my school either, but I'm sure there will probably be a time. I really don't think it's an issue about stopping prejudice, itself. It takes time. We should start by not thinking we're better than everyone else and get along with everyone like Anne Frank tried to do. Color, religion, age, culture, friends, family, etc. have nothing to do with the attitude that you bring someone. Always be polite and never make fun of anyone. Anne and her family had a lot of arguments and critical remarks but they also made up for them and got on with what they could of their so-called lives.

Carol Bell, Guntown, Mississippi

Dear Shauntae,

My name is Bill Diggs. I am a white male. I am 17. I can understand you having to hide from skinheads for six hours because I have had to hide from gangsters for three hours. I also think you have a big heart and are easy to get along with. Don't worry about prejudice because it will end one day.

Bill Diggs, Guntown, Mississippi

Dear Shauntae,

I am a white male at a pretty diverse school. I would guess it is about 80% white, 19% black, and 1% other races. I can't say that I know what it is like to have the same problem you do because I don't. I don't think one person is any better than another. Some do. It is not as bad here in Mississippi as you might think. There are still people who think they are better, but I believe every place has that in all situations. I agree that prejudices should end but as long as people are taught and raised a certain way, it is hard to change that.

Jeff Cates, Guntown, Mississippi

Dear Shauntae,

Hello! My name is Lechelle Betts. I am a black student as well. I have never faced any skinned heads in my lifetime, but I'm sure they're out there. Let's not use the word prejudice, I'd rather say racist. Now obviously you can't hide from them where you live, but I know first of all, that I couldn't go to an almost all white school myself. If you could, I suggest you move. I wish that racism would end too, but let's face it, it's not. Look, just pray and be strong, my brother, because we're all in this thing together. Hold on; be strong.

Lechelle Betts, Guntown, Mississippi

Dear Shauntae,

I don't know much about your situation, but I admire you greatly. I know that if I was in your position, I would probably feel a lot of dislike towards others. I also wouldn't be able to write about it. I know that people are still prejudiced, but to me it seems like a big waste of time. I don't understand why people spend so much time disliking people they don't even know when they could be learning from each other. I know that prejudice will never disappear, but maybe it will quiet down. It has come a long way though. My parents didn't ever attend school with different races. Now, we have people coming in from different countries.

Suzanne Segars, Guntown, Mississippi

Dear Shauntae,

I can really relate to what you are saying, but think how scary it is to hide for years and years from your own race. Being a black female going through an all black neighborhood can and will some times get you killed. Many black people are jealous of others because they can have on better shoes than them, and they will kill you and take them off your feet. It not only the skin heads or Nazis. Prejudice is everywhere.

Nikki Copeland, Guntown, Mississippi

Dear Shauntae,

I agree with you completely. Prejudice is what is ruining our world today. People thinking they are better than other people. In my eyes no matter what race you are we are all equal. If people wouldn't be like that we wouldn't have a lot of the problems we have today nor any of the problems we had in the past. I am especially thinking of Anne Frank and what happened to her. I can imagine how you must feel at your school. It must be hard feeling like an outcast and worrying about what people might say or do to you.

Summer Goff, Guntown, Mississippi

Dear Shantae,

My name is Melody Dykes. I am also black. I have never had to encounter really harsh racial problems at my school, so I can not tell you that I run in fear when I see a shaved head or a bunch of white guys grouped together. I'm not sure what a skinhead really is. They are probably just somebody who's confused about things and gets their power from making others feel low. I believe if we could just sit down with two or three skin heads and all other racial people, they would find out that their really is no dominant race. God made us all different colors and genders to see how we would react to one another and we have failed.

Melody Dykes, Guntown, Mississippi

Dear Shauntae,

My name is Darne Durden. I am 15. I am black, too. I understand your feelings although I haven't had to hide from skinheads. I feel that I have been blessed to be born black. I am a descendant of a proud people. The black race is often put down by many racists and it is very wrong through my eyes. The world is a very scary place and there are many frightening things out there. But I remember that there are many wonderful things, too. This may not help you with the skinheads, but it is at least something to think of. *Think of the wonderful things. Be proud of who you are.*

Darne Durden, Guntown, Mississippi

These responses clearly illustrate the students' serious reflection on a subject of importance and relevance to them. A few phrases from these responses stood out during our ensuing discussion that morning. The suggestion to follow Anne Frank's example and "not think we're better than everyone else" was one example. Another was Jeff Cates's noting the paradox that prejudice is "taught" to children by their elders. Melody's speculation that God had made the people of the world different "to see how we would react to one another, and we have failed" was a third. These voices would not have entered my classroom, nor would they have been heard by Shauntae and all of my students, had we not been connected to one another through telecommunications.

Online literary exchanges naturally lend themselves to the discussion and thoughtful consideration of important issues. Like the previous exchange about prejudice, there was an exchange during the first year of the conference that illustrates powerfully why these conferences should take place. That exchange, from which the next section of responses was taken, exploded into a controversial and passionate discussion of equal rights for women. With the exception of the last response, which is an example of connecting writing, this exchange most clearly illustrates the concept of reaching writing, in which the writer seeks a specific reader and, as in this case, often names that reader directly. Often, there is also elaboration on ideas and opinions, and occasionally the opinions relate to experience. A case also could be made for classifying this writing as "connecting" writing, because it often has those traits. What separates this writing from connecting writing is that although it is lively, and there is a sense of voice, the writing and opinions expressed are frequently gut-level responses, without support from the text or carefully reasoned evidence (not that the latter are generally to be expected from eighth-grade students). Many students made broad generalizations in this exchange, in an emotional response to the prompt. What is unique about this exchange is that the issue of equal rights for women is difficult, if not impossible, to discuss in the classroom without tempers and conflicts erupting. That certainly doesn't mean that it should be avoided. But, as with many other sensitive issues, such as death and dying, growing up, divorce, separation from loved ones, war, poverty, this conference provided a forum where diverse views could be expressed. The advantage of beginning a discussion in this format is that it allows for a diverse, albeit emotional, response to the issue that can then be followed up with a discussion in the classroom. After I printed out these comments and we shared them as a class by way of the overhead transparency, we had a basis for our discussion, which focused on the development and support or conflicting views of the opinions presented. It allowed us to get beyond an emotional discussion of the issue.

It is just this type of experience, in which young people use language to discuss meaningful issues in their lives in the context of literature, that is one of the driving forces behind my passion for teaching writing and literature. It is in these conversations, and in reading quality student writing, when we come as close as we can in our profession to breathing deeply as we take fresh rolls from the oven . . . knowing that they are good.

Instead of interrupting the next exchange with my analysis, here is the second half of the Nikiski prompt for the third week, followed by some of the more than thirty student responses elicited.

> As I was reading through the response log last week, I read an entry that brought up an interesting issue. Early on in the book, Anne discusses the "forwardness" of boys who blow kisses and try to hold your arm. This entry was in response to that section of the book. It was written by Theresa Petty and appears as it was written as a free write in her response log. Feel free to respond as you see fit
>
> Mr. C.
>
> Anne Frank is going through the same situation that our Jr. High goes through. Love and War might be what you call it. All of my girlfriends and I discuss who we like, and the agonizing questions of who might have a fancy for us. It's an on going cat and mouse game.
>
> I always pondered on what people meant when they said "We're going out." I thought this meant a date. Actually, in Jr. High, this means you are officially boyfriend and girlfriend. Usually this relationship only lasts a week or two. In Jr. High the average is probably three days. Soon, a heart is broken because a person has another love. then somebody gets the treatment of what is called being "dumped."
>
> In the forties, boys treated girls differently than in the nineties. Then they carried books for you, and sweetly opened the door. I think boys act different today because the women made the movement of being equal. This gave the men a different perspective of how to treat the other gender. Even though this has occurred, boys and girls will go through love sick crushes, and their hearts will beat like butterflies when the one they love walks by.
>
> What do you think about the "movement of being equal?" Have things changed? If so how? What does it mean to be "going out" in Mississippi and Vermont?
>
> Theresa Petty, Nikiski, Alaska

> I think it's great that women have made the movement of being "equal." I'm a firm believer that women can do anything a man can do. And yes, things have changed. I think more and more men realize how capable women are. Now they "allow" us to carry firewood, or they do the dishes or cook dinner for us. I think women have proved that they're just as good at sports or doing hard labor as they are. But no, we're not considered as strong as most men are, and we may not be, but we should be

allowed to at least try and show that we can do it. Here in Talkeetna "going out" means that a couple are steady with each other. But if they're just "seeing" each other, they can also go with other people also.

Tantrums Tresino, Talkeetna, Alaska

I think MEN should have MORE RIGHTS than women, because the MEN are the MONEY MAKERS in the family.

Scott Danforth, Corinth, Vermont

I agree that women should have equal rights as men. I also think that men should help women cleaning the house and cooking, but I think that women should help the men do things too.

Jayson Miller, Corinth, Vermont

Men should not have more rights because everybody should have the same rights, regardless of color, gender, or beliefs. Besides, if men had more rights than women, it can limit the powers of women job-wise. IT IS UTTERLY UNFAIR!

Rebecca Arness, Nikiski, Alaska

Gene, I guess you're a boy. I am too, but I'd like to know why you think men should have more rights? I totally agree on women having the same rights. But, if a lady can't do something even close to as good as a guy, I think she should either do something else, where instead women decide to sue or be irrational. I think this goes for men and for women.

Daniel Smith, Nikiski, Alaska

I agree with Tantrums Tresino about men and women being equal. I think women should be paid as much as men if they're doing the same job. In business they pay women less for doing a "man's job." That is just not fair, especially if they do a better job at it. I know some things are meant for only men, like football, but women and men should share chores like cooking, cleaning and anything like that.

Ashley Gambrell, Guntown, Mississippi

I, Jason and my friend Brad, have to disagree with your response (that men and women should be treated equally). We're not saying that women can't do a job as well as men, but we were brought up believing that women shouldn't have to carry firewood or anything heavy. What we're trying to say is that it is polite for a man to help a lady with her load. Women CAN do those things, but we believe they shouldn't have to.

Jason Murell and Brad Bird, Nikiski, Alaska

> In our opinion you are partly right and partly wrong. For example, if you had a non-working wife who had babies, then the children should come first and she should have dinner started or something defrosting (not everything done.) Maybe he could come home and help cook dinner or watch the kids. On the other hand, if she has no kids and nothing to do, she should have no reason not to have any dinner ready.
>
> Holly Petty and Amber Hansen, Nikiski, Alaska

> I think that men in the 40's were more polite and considerate to their female partners. A way that could solve the problems today would be that no certain person could have more control than another. People today need to talk with each other more.
>
> Christy R., Guntown, Mississippi

> I don't think men should give women any special treatment like opening doors just because they are women. All people are the same, I think.
>
> Rose Young, Guntown, Mississippi

As we discussed the prompt and the responses as they came in, the discussion in my classroom was highly animated, almost to the point of chaos. As Peggy Turner commented in one of her messages: "This got pretty wild. How does one solve the battle of the sexes?" My one regret is that even though the issue was brought up, discussed, written about, and processed with further discussion, students could not create fully developed, reasoned essays because of the pace of the conference in that first year. I would have preferred that my students had written short formal responses to the original prompt, supporting their opinions with evidence, from either experience or outside sources, in logical, reasoned statements. Fortunately, in the third year of the conference, a formal essay as a cumulative writing assignment was added as a part of the sequence. After reading Annabeth's essay, I decided that the writing, although it was often wonderful, was not taken completely through a revision process during the conference. We now spend a few weeks at the end of the sequence for a formal personal essay, selecting one issue or quote from the text or the conference to use as a basis, as we did for Jenny's essay (see Chapter 6).

If there was a defining moment in the equal rights discussion it was when we read the following response by one of Peggy Turner's students.

> This is the 90's people, wake up! The boys in our class (some of them) have this idea in their heads that men are more superior than women. We argued a lot on how a family should be . . . I just

think it is wonderful for the women to have equal rights. Women do not stay home and keep the house running and wear aprons. We WORK. We have jobs in factories, offices, and everywhere. We have important things to tend to. We do not come every time some of you men ring your little bells for us!

Jessica Kolb, Guntown, Mississippi

In these two exchanges on prejudice and equal rights, students are writing to one another. How does this represent significant change for my classroom? How does this exchange fit into the big picture of school reform that we read and hear so much about? For my students and me, there were several aspects of this experience that are quite different from the type of tasks that usually occupied our days. First, it is the students who determined the content of the writing. It was the class in Guntown who initiated this conversation by asking about prejudice. It was Theresa Petty who initiated the discussion about equal rights. Second, the experience was relevant to students because of its pertinence in their lives and in our society. And third, the students had ownership in this process because they made real decisions about what happened and how it happened. This is truly a student-centered network, in which students can make real decisions about their learning. A classroom of mostly white students in Alaska heard diverse viewpoints from other students of the same age. Shauntae in particular found a real purpose and audience for his writing. He discovered that, although he was part of a very small minority in Nikiski, a multitude of others shared similar experiences in the world at large. As a teacher, I see firsthand what happens when these factors come together in a school setting. Although many of these discoveries have taken place in my classroom at other times, I've learned that the exchange is a powerful tool that will appear again in my classroom. It might be a part of one of the large, top-down, initiatives that are happening, such as technical preparation, year-round schooling, long-block scheduling, and the Alaska 2000 initiative. Was this a big idea, affecting students throughout our school, our district, the state? Certainly not. However, in considering the exchange's importance, I recalled the following passage from "A Small Good Thing" by Raymond Carver.

"You probably need to eat something," the baker said. "I hope you'll eat some of my hot rolls. You have to eat and keep going. Eating is a small, good thing in a time like this," he said (120–121).

Was this exchange a "small, good thing" for my students, an example of real reform? I think so. And, "in a time like this," when talk shows are spewing hatred, when "The Contract For America" is draining funds for education and other social programs while increasing defense spending (again), and when politicians are stirring up racial tensions by blaming immigrants for our economic problems, it is these efforts that matter. In our state thousands of dollars have been spent creating standards for all of the content areas K-12. Groups of teachers, parents, community members, school board members, and others have spent an immense sum working on the standards and presenting them to the public in a variety of ways. I worked hard as a member of one of these groups on the Language Arts standards, which were eventually adopted by the Alaska State School Board and the state legislature. We then spent days and days reviewing and adjusting them for our local district. Soon, they too will be approved. Within a few weeks each teacher will find a copy in the school mailbox. The principals will hold a faculty meeting and explain how these standards will change the face of education as we know it. The teachers will politely leave the meeting and place them in a cupboard, in a drawer, or in the trash—wherever it is that they put these things that are handed down from above.

One thing I have learned in education is that the trickle-down theory of school reform doesn't work. The only real change that happens in classrooms is a result either of teachers learning from their students or of teachers learning from other teachers. I learned a valuable lesson with this experience. I realized the incredible power of telecommunications to affect my students' lives. Shauntae walked out of my room a different person after reading those responses and participating in the discussion that followed. In a time when it is easy, tempting, and safe to close our doors and keep to ourselves, it is more important than ever to join the much larger classroom without walls that technology has brought to us.

8 Inhabiting the Consequences of Our Work

There are two remaining critical questions that must be addressed after having presented and discussed the emergence of this new literacy, this unique form of discourse that happens during online literary exchanges. First, how does this literacy fit into the lives of teachers? What are the implications for teaching, learning, professional development, and collaboration? Second, how does this literacy fit into students' lives? What does this mean for my eighth-grade students as they move into high school and enter the adult world? These are complex questions, but, after closely studying what happened during the first three years of the Anne Frank Conference, I'd like to speculate on the implications of this new step in the evolution of literacy.

Where does this literacy fit into the lives of teachers? To answer this key question, I have to begin with collaboration. As a teacher, I've been somewhat fortunate in terms of collaboration. Unlike many teachers who are isolated from other teachers, I've had many opportunities to work with my peers. When I began teaching in Nunapitchuk, there were only nine certified teachers, and collaboration and integration were a matter of necessity. I worked as a language arts specialist in a K-2 school where I worked on a rotating basis in ten different classrooms with ten teachers who had very different approaches to literacy learning. Through professional organizations like the Alaska State Writing Consortium and the Alaska Teacher Research Network, I've been involved in several collaborative professional projects. More recently, as a team leader of an interdisciplinary team in a middle school for five years, I collaborated daily with my peers to plan interdisciplinary curriculum. Yet, in all of these experiences, I didn't grow as significantly as a teacher or make as many significant steps forward in my thinking about teaching as I did as a result of this project.

What happened when the Anne Frank Conference teachers collaborated online? Significantly, this collaboration did not turn into a forum for complaining and despair, as it easily could have. Despite all the bad press, the funding inequities, the lack of technology, the lack of parental support, and on and on, we as teachers still have the sacred opportunity to spend our days in rooms full of bright young people. Even though we have very difficult jobs, and as rural teachers are often asked to do more than any reasonable person would expect to be possible in a school day, the "teacher talk" in the conference was overwhelmingly positive. There were frustrations that we can learn from, and these were voiced. But, like Mary's story in the first section, the conference was also an avenue to share our victories.

Teachers learn best by looking closely at students as learners, readers, and writers. It is from this learning that we should develop our pedagogy, our curriculum, and our assessment. Such learning should be the foundation of everything we do, and it can't be done in isolation. We have to share our learning with other teachers and administrators, as well as with the public. This doesn't have to take the form of a teacher-research project, such as this book, or a formal professional article for *English Journal*. In fact, it is sometimes the informal "teacher talk" we engage in that has the greatest impact. During the three years of the conference on which this book is based, a rich layer of conversation surrounded the student work online and in our classrooms. One of my favorite pieces of writing from that time is the following response, written by a serious and gifted learner, teacher Peggy Turner.

> Cara and Tammy,
>
> Let us remember that childhood is usually the only time of innocence and freedom where play and "one day at a time" living is valued and permissible. Tragedy robs children of childhood and forces on them a life of worry and heaviness that they would not have to bear in a perfect world.
>
> Ms. Turner

Aside from the beauty of the language that Peggy Turner uses, isn't this a wonderful way for a teacher to talk to a student? Can it compare to a letter grade, or to the number of mistakes marked on the top of a page? This is real stuff. There were several instances where Peggy "spoke" directly to students during the conference.

In addition to the occasional teacher-to-student response, there were many teacher-to-teacher exchanges throughout the conference each year. I've classified those exchanges for the first year alone, listing the number of times they occurred in the conference, to give you a feel for the types of teacher-to-teacher discussions that were happening. The teacher talk was about: pedagogy (20), materials and texts (9), logistics, technology, prompts (23), text/content (10), student observations (27), and other, such as questions, article talk, and so on (16). I should point out two things. First, many messages went directly from one teacher to another and did not go through the conference and are not a part of the transcript; there were also several phone calls, as well as exchanges of materials through the mail. As a result of this teacher sharing, I now have three bulging manila folders in my files with supporting materials, such as articles about the Holocaust, prereading activities, newspaper clippings, fiction, and poetry. Originally I had classified which responses were to individual teachers and which were to the group as a whole. Since the messages were predominantly to everyone, I don't think it is necessary to differentiate. The following sections present one example from each teacher talk category.

1. Pedagogy

> Mary, I don't understand what you mean by the timeline. Do I have it? Explain. I have a teaching committee set up—two or three from each class who are reading Anne Frank now and meeting to discuss ideas that come to them for possible exchanges, emphasizing that this is new and exciting business and I need their help and ideas. I want their input as to what should be covered. (I am discovering how very structured we are in our school—I am finding it impossible to meet with this team—there is no free time. I am beginning to think that is a good sign though. When we start having new problems like this, it means something new is going on.)
>
> Peggy Turner

Where can discussions such as this take place in the traditional rural school setting? The few moments at the photocopy machine with the high school English teacher or the basketball coach won't suffice. When Mary, Sondra, Tom, and I read pieces like this, we connected with teachers on common ground, a rare event for rural teachers. When I read passages like this, it occurred to me that for the first time in nine years of teaching I was hearing from a rural teacher who had students the same age as mine, and who also had a similar number of students (more than one hundred) who were about to engage with the same text, at the same time. When I walked into my classroom, it was if there were five teachers and their expertise coming together. The terrible sense of isolation and the nagging question of "Am I doing this right and does anybody care?" were gone. After reading Peggy's note, I took the idea of a teaching committee to our team meeting, and we vowed to invite students to our team meetings to assist with planning interdisciplinary activities.

The next exchanges refer to the nitty-gritty, the nuts and bolts of the conference. The first is an excerpt from the notes from our audio conference planning session, posted by Sondra.

2. Materials

> A recommended book by Mary is *Anne Frank: Beyond the Diary*. This is available from the Dartmouth Book Store and Mary has already posted the number . . . Another appropriate novel suggested is Jane Yolen's *The Devil's Arithmetic* . . . Caroline (Eisner) has volunteered to go the Holocaust Museum in DC and look for resources.
>
> Sondra Porter

The book *Anne Frank: Beyond the Diary* is incredible. It has color photos of the actual diary, of the annex, of food ration coupons, of the officer who raided the annex and arrested the Franks, and of the records that show the Frank family leaving for the camps. Perhaps of greatest significance are the numerous photos of Anne and the Frank family from vacations and holidays. The book makes the people in the diary come alive in a historical family album. When my students were reading the diary, I waited until we had been at it for a week or so before I pulled out *Beyond the Diary*. There was always stunned silence as I opened the book to show evidence that we were not reading fiction. This one note from Sondra made an impact on several classes. I think we all purchased *Anne Frank: Beyond the Diary* and *The Devil's Arithmetic*, which were particularly accessible for the lower-skilled readers. Caroline also mailed out an extensive packet of materials from the Holocaust Museum, including an excellent bibliography of resources.

3. Technology/Pedagogy

> Our electronic classroom connection has changed the work my students are doing this year because they have a new audience and an authentic reason for writing. They are no longer writing for the teacher. (My students have mostly been together since kindergarten and they are ready to fly up to the high school.) This project gives them the chance to spread those wings, but still remain in the safety of good ole Waits River Valley School for a while longer. The kids are eager to write and bemoan the fact that their time is limited (on the computer). Several students come in during their lunch hour to write on the disk. They and I feel the rest of the kids in project are REAL. Each classroom seems to have a personality that comes through over the Bread-Net. That's amazing to us. We think that even if you didn't label your entries, we would know who was "talking." One of the things that helps this along is the picture of each of you teachers that I took this summer and refer to frequently. . . .
>
> Mary Burnham

In reading Mary's letter, I am again struck by the similarity of our experience. Despite the fact that our students were literally thousands of miles apart, and very different culturally as well, the conference's impact on their literacy had strong common threads. Obviously this project was about more than technology. You can see that it was an interesting process to classify these exchanges. Because the nature of teaching is complex, so is writing about it. I think the "personality" that came through with each class is due to several factors. There is a local dialect, particularly from the students in Mississippi; but we also saw words in the conference from Alaska, particularly slang, that were not common in the Lower Forty-Eight. Even though Mary's entry was written just halfway through the conference (during the third week), it was indicative of what we were all thinking and seeing by then. Something unique was happening.

4. Text/Content

> The displays sound great to me. Several strong images haunt me—a child's small black coat with a yellow star, those hand-sewn curtains pieced together by Pim and Anne and gathered on a string. What else? . . .
>
> Peggy Turner

In this note Peggy is commenting on and embellishing the idea of a display that my students had created for the library.

5. Student Observations

> I agree with Sondra and Scott that the kids are more responsive to the prompts than the book itself, BUT my kids are going back to the book to read more deeply because of the prompts . . . at least many of them are. They are borrowing the book over the weekend etc. (Oh yes, I had to borrow enough copies from the high school and sign my name in blood to return them in good condition, but I only have enough for one class at a time.)
>
> Mary Burnham

I remember a phone conversation with Sondra about halfway through the project. We talked about how to manage the reading (fast readers, slow readers, and non-readers; reading out loud and reading independently) and how to manage the writing (in journals on the computer, individually or in groups; to be published or not to be published). We discussed the students' reactions to the book, our frustrations with handling so much writing, and explaining to the kids why they didn't always have a personal response to everything they wrote. I called because I had an uneasy feeling that maybe the other classrooms were having a different kind of experience. Even though we discussed these things online, I needed to talk "live" about what was happening. Naturally the conversation moved into other areas . . . our administrators, our assessment policy . . . absenteeism . . . you name it. Although all participating teachers didn't talk with one another by phone regularly, the few occasions when we did were very fruitful. If the layer of teacher talk had been removed from the conference, this would have been an entirely different experience for me as a teacher, and for my students. It is in such teacher talk that we as teachers process our theory through the reality of our experience in the classroom.

After the first two years of the conference, during which the participating teachers were basically the same each year (with the addition of Helena Fagan the second year), there was a great deal of interest in the Bread Loaf Rural Teacher Network's Anne Frank Conference. During the fall of 1995 there were about two dozen teachers who expressed interest in participating. Since the volume of responses with five classrooms involved already had bordered on becoming unmanageable, there was no way that this many additional teachers could participate in the same format. So, after a general call was made for interested teachers, the large group was divided into three sub-groups; each sub-group would have a "read-only" folder within the Anne Frank Conference, meaning that anyone with BreadNet access could read the files in the conference, but only the participating teachers could post their student writing there. In Group Two, I was the only teacher who had had previous experience with the conference. After some preliminary dialogue about timelines and structure, we were up and rolling. The participants would be Les Fortier and Patricia Parrish from Mississippi, Phil Sittnick from New Mexico, and myself. Sheri Skelton had expressed interest but was unable to join because her book order failed to reach her remote Alaskan site. Just before the first week's prompt was posted, Phil sent the following letter to the planning folder.

> Hi Y'all:
>
> We're about 50 pages into the book so far, we've spent about 7 class periods reading. We have to read the book in class together, for a couple of reasons: 1) I only have one set (30 books) and 3 classes of about 24 each, and, 2) only a few of my students would do the reading if I assigned it. Basically, we've got to read the whole thing aloud together in class if I want all the students to get it. So, that's what we're doing.

Anyway, what the reality check's about: my students are reacting rather unfavorably to the book. Given that "This is boring" is a middle school battle cry, one that is heard throughout the land, not just at LMS or in my classroom, I'm sure, they are still having a hard time with this because there's so little action. They like action. They're complaining rather vigorously.

So, I've been trying my best to answer their question which deserves a good answer: "Why do we have to read this?"

I've told them: because we're going to read SOMETHING in this class; we have the opportunity to share our feelings about the book with other students using BreadNet if we read THIS book; it's written by someone who was your peer; it has a lot of reflection and thought representative of adolescence; it explores topics which are very relevant even today, and especially to you guys (all Native Americans), like racism and genocide; and it teaches us about an extremely important event in history: the Holocaust. These are the main reasons I've given them for reading Anne Frank.

Still, there's a lot of whining each day when we read, and they get agitated and restless after about 20-25 minutes (our periods are 47 minutes). I know that they'll be much more into it when we start to exchange writing—we're signed up for some 15 days in the computer lab over the next 6 weeks, so we'll be able to respond, and break up the reading that way. Still, I'm curious, as a teacher who's just reading Anne Frank with his students for the first time: are my students' reactions typical? My answers to their questions? How do you all handle their negativity?

Be advised that I'm already getting part of the answer, when I read about the context-building activities Patricia is doing— the "What we know, what we want to know" stuff, guest speakers, videos, library research, etc. I'm sure that these activities help build interest and understanding. But, how do your students react to the text itself?

Phil Sittnick

Phil's letter was like a flashback to my first year of teaching the book. I had been so excited about the new telecommunications exchange. We had created a display in the library; we had watched some films and had studied World War II to set the stage. Then we started the book and I experienced the same basic reaction that Phil described. Here is my response to Phil.

Dear Phil,

Thank you for sending your honest appraisal of what is happening in your classroom. The teaching of the diary has gone through quite an evolution in my classroom, as I ran into some of the same resistance you speak of. First off, I think it helps to view the text as a collection of short pieces instead of as a unified narrative like a novel. It's perfectly okay in my book to skip an entry or two to keep things moving. Also, I have a variety of things happening every day other than the reading. Each student has a response notebook where they respond to specific quotes and issues raised in the text. These mainly derive from the three areas of focus in Anne's writing: her own emotional/psychological state and growth, the interactions of people within the annex and lastly, the world outside of the annex. We are also studying the vocabulary from context, as much of the reading is hard for my kids. We do a variety of games and activities centered around words that are unfamiliar to them. The kids are also creating bulletin boards by bringing in photos, drawings, poems . . . anything related to Anne Frank, WWII and the Holocaust. We also dramatize small portions of the entries, with impromptu role playing scenes at the front of the room. The most important part of the sequence so far has been the social studies teacher's intro to the historical period. You're probably asking yourself how you can do all of these kinds of things and still read the book by the end of the year. My suggestion is to read ahead, and perhaps skip a few of the "daily business" entries. This will lessen the dramatic impact of the ending to some degree, but it will keep things moving. I hate to admit breaking the law, but when I only had one class set, I photocopied the entire book in forty-page segments and passed them out. My only other idea would be to see if there is another teacher who has these kids who would collaborate with you to bring the text into context with videos, other readings, drama, etc. . . . I'm going to be reading my first round of response notebooks this week, so I'll have a better idea how it's going. The discussion has been good so far. Hang in there!

We'll be posting our first prompt tomorrow (Monday).

Scott

Many things happen in an exchange like this. First we have to identify what it is that is troubling us (or exciting or confusing us) about what is happening in the classroom. Then we have to sit down and write about it. This act in itself is very worthwhile and often yields fruit in terms of ideas for possible solutions. Furthermore, when we sit down to consider what another teacher has written, in a different situation, but in a similar context, it renders insight into our pedagogy and our situations.

This chapter is called "Inhabiting the Consequences of Our Work." To me, it doesn't do any good to read professional journals, to go to conferences, to collaborate, to innovate, to put our energy into teaching, if we as teachers are not going to learn from what we do and apply this learning to our teaching. For too long, the primary sources of learning for teachers have been degree programs and courses for recency credit or salary advancement, taught by university people who, at best, are many years removed from the classroom, or, at worst, have never had a full-time teaching position in a public school. It is high time that teachers across the country begin to do serious, deliberate research in their classrooms and to share the knowledge they gain with other teachers. A book like Nancie Atwell's *In the Middle, Reading and Writing with Adolescents* has had more real impact on teaching than any other event, program, or "system" to be passed down from the universities.

This book is a learning journey for me. Each day as I write I come away with another view of what has happened here, another perspective of what this experience was like for a particular student or teacher. This learning is worthwhile in and of itself. But I'm also hoping that the insights here will guide my teaching practice in the future and be helpful to other teachers. An example of a teacher beginning to "inhabit the consequences of his work" is this letter from Phil, written toward the end of the conference. The first step toward learning from our students is purposeful, systematic reflection on what has happened.

> Hey Everyone:
>
> We finally finished ANNE FRANK: THE DIARY OF A YOUNG GIRL. There was great relief to be done with the book—it's been a difficult one for my students to get through enjoyably. At the same time, everybody got a bit choked up at the epilogue and the afterword, which described Anne's fate after they were found in hiding. I could sense more than a few lumps in throats around the room (including my own). It was a touching moment for me (and them); it's rare that I've seen literature have that profound of an effect on my students. That moment made the whole effort of getting through the book worthwhile.
>
> Of course, telecommunicating with you all has also made it a very special experience, too. I've noticed a lot of growth in my students' writing in the last few weeks—more than I've ever seen during the course of a single unit. They're using new vocabulary: respond, response, prompt, etc. But more importantly, they're starting to come out of their shells a bit reading. Having an audience of peers to communicate with has been critical for this to occur, I'm convinced, because I've asked them many times to respond to me, and often they have nothing to say to me about what they've read. It's helped them to see that there isn't always just ONE right answer, and that it doesn't hurt to risk an opinion. I think they'll be much better prepared to respond to literature now, in a variety of contexts.
>
> We're off for a week of Spring Break after tomorrow (Friday, March 15). We'll be on to something new when we return (we're

going to be studying raptors for awhile). Feel free to drop us a line, though—comments, questions, or just staying in touch—my students will have continuing access to computers with some ability to respond to you.

Again, we've enjoyed the conference—hope you all have, too.

Phil Sittnick

Phil wrote this from his perspective as a teacher at Laguna Middle School, on the Laguna Pueblo Indian Reservation. Phil's students not only have the traditional challenges in literacy that all adolescents face, they also have cultural and linguistic hurdles to climb as they attempt to function in the language of modern Western society. In addition to cultural considerations, there are countless variables to consider when determining "growth" in writing. It is virtually impossible to isolate one event or procedure in a causal relationship with a change in a student's literacy habits. But, for me as a teacher, Phil's second paragraph, about students "coming out of their shells" and recognizing that there "isn't always just ONE right answer," is very telling; Phil is not the type of person to misrepresent what happens in his classroom. Knowing that most teachers tend to be overly critical of their practice and to dwell on the areas of concern instead of success, I find that there is no more credible voice than a teacher telling a classroom story. We will look closely at a few of the students' experiences from Phil's room in a moment, but first I want to consider the larger question. Where does this literacy fit into student's lives? As we've seen through the writing presented in this book, adolescence is a tumultuous and difficult time. As Nancie Atwell pointed out in *In the Middle: Reading and Writing and Learning with Adolescents*, it is our job as teachers not to ignore the unique attributes of our students, or to try to subvert them, but to incorporate this uniqueness into our teaching.

> First, teachers of junior high have to accept the reality of junior high students. Confusion, bravado, restlessness, a preoccupation with peers, and the questioning of authority are not manifestations of poor attitude; they are the hallmarks of this particular time of life. By nature adolescents are volatile and social, and our teaching can take advantage of this, helping kids find meaningful ways to channel their energies and social needs instead of trying to legislate against them. (p. 25)

What better way to take advantage of the social needs of our students than to connect their study of literature and writing to other students? Annabeth, Jenny, Joel, and all the students involved in the exchange were motivated by an opportunity not only to create a new self, but to engage in a meaningful social situation, one of the most desirable activities for an adolescent. What does this exchange mean for students? I hope that they have discovered that communicating with others about serious issues, including literature, can be as rewarding as conversations about what happened last weekend and sharing "secrets you make at midnight" (as Jenny Anderson said).

In terms of their literacy development, I concur with the latest thinking about reading and writing being constructivist activities. Through this new electronic "zone of proximal development," to use Vygotsky's term, students are creating meaning. In their essay, "Toward a Composing Model of Reading," Robert J. Tierney and P. David Pearson begin with the essence of this notion.

> We believe that at the heart of understanding reading and writing connections one must begin to view reading and writing as essentially similar processes of meaning construction. Both are acts of composing. From a reader's perspective, meaning is created as a reader uses his background of experience together with the author's cues to come to grips both with what the writer is getting him to do or think and what the reader decides and creates for himself. As a writer writes, she uses her own background of experience to generate ideas and, in order to produce a text which is considerate to her idealized reader, filters these drafts through her judgments about what her reader's background of experience will be, what she wants to say and what she wants to get the reader to think or do. In a sense both reader and writer must adapt to their perceptions about their partner in negotiating what a text means. (p. 261)

If we apply this idea to a telecommunications exchange, students are composing meaning on both ends of the discussion, the level of concern about the audience and their understanding of the text is raised considerably, and so is the efficacy of the writing. The writing in this conference was better than what I had seen in other informal responses to literature because students were aware, *while they were composing*, of the fact that other students were going to be making meaning out of their writing. Students would refer to the text, the dictionary, the teacher and each other to clarify and to sharpen their meaning before sending it off. Eighth graders are not innately inclined to revise their writing; that holds true for most people. We would all prefer that our readers love every word we have written and that they understand the subtlest and most obscure of our thoughts. It takes a specific purpose, an increased awareness of the outcome of our meaning making, to force us to shape and refine our message. In terms of students' literacy, I'd like to suggest that for many students this was the first time that they had made a serious investment in their writing, revising and clarifying their ideas when it was not "legislated" by the teacher. Does this mean that from now on my students will continue to revise and to invest in their writing, anticipating the reader's understanding of their work and moving beyond their own intuitive sense of what their words mean? I wouldn't say that this will happen, but I would emphatically say that after discovering the power of this process they are more likely to do so.

We'll look more specifically at the actual literacy development that happens for individual students when we look later at Phil's classroom experiences. But first, we need to return to the diary, where Anne's analysis of her life compels us to think about our students' lives and how these young people change as they grow up. Here, in one of the most mature and sophisticated entries from the diary, Anne talks about her new "self-consciousness."

Saturday, July 15, 1944

Dear Kitty,

We have had a book from the library with the challenging title of: What Do You Think of the Modern Young Girl? I want to talk about this subject today.

The author of this book criticizes "the youth of today" from top to toe, without, however, condemning the whole of the young brigade as "incapable of anything good." On the contrary she is rather of the opinion that if young people wished, they have it in their hands to make a bigger, more beautiful and better world, but that they occupy themselves with superficial things, without giving a thought to real beauty.

In some passages, the writer gave me very much the feeling she was directing her criticism at me, and that's why I want to lay myself completely bare to you for once and defend myself against this attack.

I have one outstanding trait in my character, which must strike anyone who knows me for any length of time, and that is my knowledge of myself. I can watch myself and my actions, just like an outsider. The Anne of every day I can face entirely without prejudice, without making excuses for her and watch what's good and what's bad about her. This "self-consciousness" haunts me, and every time I open my mouth I know as soon as I've spoken whether "that ought to have been different": or "that was right as it was." There are so many things about myself that I condemn; I couldn't begin to name them all. I understand more and more how true Daddy's words were when he said: "All children must look after their own upbringing." Parents can only give good advice or put them on the right paths, but the final forming of a person's character lies in their own hands.

In addition to this, I have lots of courage, I always feel so strong as if I can bear a great deal, I feel so free and so young! I was glad when I first realized it, because I don't think I shall easily bow down before the blows that inevitably come to everyone.

Considering the fact that this entry was written just eight months before Anne Frank perished at Bergen Belsen, there is a profound irony to this last paragraph. But aside from the poignancy of the knowledge that the articulate, sensitive, poetic voice of this young woman came to a tragic end, I see in this passage the realization of my most ambitious and valued goal as a teacher. Like Anne, I desire for my students to have "self-consciousness" as readers, as writers, as citizens of their community, and as human beings in charge of their destiny. The knowledge that "the final forming of one's character lies in their own hands" is the single most important idea that students can take from my classroom. There has always been talk in education about metacognition—the knowledge of one's own learning processes—and the old saying about teaching someone to fish instead of giving them the fish, and so on. I'm talking about a much larger concept here: personal responsibility for growing your "self," as a learner, and as a human being. Some of my students come from wonderful, caring, nurturing families, where they are taught about responsibility and decision making and values. Some of my students are literally raising themselves; their parents, who often work at the oil fields on the North Slope for weeks on end, are caught in a pattern of abusing substances or are simply not in the picture. Regardless of what is happening outside the school, this message, that Anne so clearly articulated, is the one I want my students to take with them when they leave my classroom: this is *your* life.

Where does this literacy fit into students' lives? I think that, for many students, their experience with the Anne Frank Conference, and the ensuing development for them as readers, writers, and individuals, will give them more confidence and greater skill with language. Through the recognition that there is a world beyond their classroom, their school, their community, and their own period in history, these students will be better equipped to adapt to new situations as they arise, and to articulate their visions of those changes, both within themselves and the world at large.

Perhaps that is why I found this experience—reading the diary, writing about the diary and responding to other student writing through telecommunications, discussing the issues that arise—to be so pedagogically, developmentally, and philosophically sound for me as a teacher. As Anne Frank grows from a self-centered, silly, somewhat materialistic young girl, to a sophisticated, worldly, mature young woman, I found myself looking at my own beliefs and perceptions of myself and the people around me, just as I was hoping that my students would. Likewise, I was growing and learning as a teacher through the power of this collaboration.

We've seen how this literacy fits into teacher's lives in important ways: it helps us to be better teachers, better learners in our classroom, and happier, more confident people with the support of kind, generous colleagues from around the country. I'd like this presentation of the project and the speculation about what it all means to be an impetus for more talk about the emerging literacy that is happening as a result of this technology; perhaps, there will be more support for the emerging notion of our students as people who can be trusted and encouraged to take over their own learning. As teachers read this book I hope they will come away with a renewed commitment, not only to promoting students' self-consciousness of their learning processes, and their lives in general, but to increasing *their own self-consciousness* about our profession while taking the time and energy to share that learning with others.

Before I discuss the responses that follow, I'll repeat my ritual disclaimer about my evaluation of student writing. You are free to come to your own conclusions after looking at this writing. I am merely offering my observations and speculations based on my experience as a teacher, reader, writer, and participant in this conference. The responses in this section were selected based on the following criteria: (1) all the writing is from Phil Sittnick's class (because I wanted to see if I could get a sense of the growth in terms of literacy development that Phil described in his letter); (2) all the responses are from the same students but were written at different times—early in the conference and later as the conference developed. In addition, I wanted responses that were interesting to read and could stand alone, not dependent on other writing for their meaning. Since this chapter is about inhabiting the consequences of our work, I also wanted to find responses that evoked the energy and spirit of the conference in order to discuss the larger implications for this work. In the next section, the responses are organized in sets of writings from the same student. The first of each set was posted on February 5 in response to the following prompt from Nikiski, Alaska.

January 31

The 8th-grade students at Nikiski Middle School would like to ask the other students participating in the Anne Frank Conference to respond to either or both of these prompts. The first is from Mr. Christian's second-hour class; the second one is from third hour. We sent a copy to your mailboxes to make sure everyone received this. From now on, we'll send to the conference only. Happy Writing!

1. From the entry: Monday, 7 December 1942

"Then I fall asleep with a stupid feeling of wishing to be different from what I am or from what I want to be; perhaps to behave differently from the way I want to behave, or do behave."

Who would Anne like to be? How does this quote relate to your own life?

2. From the entry: Friday July 23, 1943

"Just for fun I'm going to tell you each person's first wish, when we are allowed to go outside again. Margot and Mr. Van Daan long more than anything for a hot bath filled to overflowing and want to stay in it for half an hour. Mrs. Van Daan wants most to go and eat cream cakes immediately. Dussel thinks of nothing but seeing his wife . . . Mummy of her cup of coffee; Daddy is going to visit Mr. Vossen first; Peter the town and a cinema while I should find it so blissful, I shouldn't know where to start! But most of all, I long for a home of our own, to be able to move freely and to have some help with my work again at last, in other words—school."

If you were to come out of hiding after a long time, what would you do first?

The second response from each student occurred later in the conference.

February 5

Dear Students,

I think Anne would like to be someone like you and me because she did not get to have any fun like the way kids are supposed to. Instead her and her family had to hide in a building called the "Secret Annex" because of what was going on back then.

If I were to come out of hiding for a long time, then the first thing I would do is I would go back to school and get my education that I would need for the future. Then after that I would go and see all my friends (if they're still alive) and then visit the place where I used to live.

Sincerely,

Lorelei Pino, 8th grader at Laguna Middle School

February 21

I would go somewhere where I wouldn't have to worry about anything. Like I'd go to a tropical island in the middle of the ocean, but not exactly in the middle of the ocean. Because something bad might happen and then I'll be stuck there forever.

A perfect mother would be someone who cares about me, and lets me go anywhere as long as it sounds right to her and tells me what's right and what's wrong. A perfect mother would also be someone I could tell other stuff. Yes, I think my Mom does live up to that image, because she cares for me a lot and worries about what I did and always wants to spend time with me on my birthday, or even on special holidays.

Lorelei Pino, Laguna, New Mexico

I see two aspects of this writing that evolved from the first response to the second. First, in the initial response, Lorelei's first piece of writing to be posted in the conference, there is a certain hesitancy, a somewhat passive voice, a lack of personal investment. She has answered the question, but there isn't a solid sense of Lorelei in the writing. This entry is similar to the performing and reaching writing that we discussed earlier. There is little mark of the individual writer present. When we look at the second response, we see a relaxing of the writerly navigator. Lorelei has turned her imagination loose to present a tropical island. Moreover, the second paragraph is personal. She's not just talking about an abstract notion of motherhood, she's talking about her mother, and the image she aspires to. There is a clear sense of voice in the second piece. If I were to classify this piece, it would fall into the connecting writing category. The closing is simply "Lorelei Pino," a less formal closing than "Sincerely, Lorelei Pino, 8th Grader at Laguna Middle School." My overall impression is that Lorelei has become more comfortable, more open with her writing online.

Feb. 5

Hello, my name is Bobbie Tsosie-Hohenstein and I am reading the diary of Anne Frank in Mr. Sittnick's 6th period. My opinion about this book is I personally think that Anne was a very bright and gifted young lady. She had a mind of her own. Whatever she thought she would put it down in writing, and that was her way of speaking. So far the book is OK at first. I didn't really enjoy it; but it is getting pretty good. Well, to answer your questions I think Anne would want to be a person without worries and to do things right without getting yelled at because people are always getting mad at her and correcting her for everything she does. Sometimes I wish that I was someone else because in my life I have a lot of difficulties but I've learned to overcome them. Well, if I just got out of hiding after a long time, I would go to all my friends and family's houses and talk to them and ask them how they are doing and tell them how the family is, and I would go and get a big pizza and a big Dr. Pepper.

Bobbie Tsosie-Hohenstein, Laguna, New Mexico

March 11

Dear Students at Stringer, Mississippi,

Hello, my name is Bobbie Tsosie-Hohenstein and I am in the 8th grade at Laguna Middle School. I am 14 years old and I live in a little village called Seama. It is one 6 villages in Laguna. Well, to answer your questions: which one of the people would you most like to be? I think that I would like to be Miep because I like to help people and I am very friendly toward others. I do not put myself before others. Well, that is all I have to say so bye-bye.

Only me,

Bobbie

One of the things that I love about my job is that no two days, no two periods, and—most of all—no two students are alike. I included these two responses because I think Bobbie took to this conference like a fish to water. She jumped in and started swimming. Her first response is lively and personal. It is clearly connected to the text and the prompts that arose from the reading. She is thinking about Anne's life and writing in comparison to his own. I also love the last line. Throughout my analysis of the work that happened in the conference, I am continually reminded that these students are not undergraduates. They are adolescents being themselves. For many of them, there is no greater joy than pizza and a pop. In Bobbie's second entry, she was the only student I noticed who wished to be Miep. Her closing is also touching in a way, as if she is acknowledging that she is not a literary critic, nor a telecommunications expert, "only" a student saying what she thinks.

In the next set of writings, the student's first response answers Nikiski's prompt questions in inverse order.

February 5

Dear Students,

   Hi, my name is Jennifer Lucas. I am from Laguna, N.M. I would like to tell you what I would do first.

Q. #2 Well if I was coming out of a hiding place for that long I would probably go back to school and catch up on my studying. Most of you think I must be crazy to go back to school but the reason why I am going to do this is because I wouldn't want to fall too far behind as I would be. Then again, I would also go back to see some of my friends. That is really what I would do, how about you?

Q.#1 Well I think Anne would like to be like her sister because her sister can really do anything she would like. She can read books and Anne can't, so she has to read them in the attic where nobody will find her. She has to do this on her free time and her sister gets more respect from Mrs. Van Daan. I don't really think this quote relates anything to my life because I wouldn't want to be anything like my sister, because she is always getting in trouble with her school work and the people she hangs around with. I got just about all I need and not much more. Well that is all I got to write so until you write or type back.

Jennifer's second writing responds not only to the second prompt, but also to a comment from Travis Taylor (from Kurt Broderson's class in Vermont, who participated briefly in the third year of the conference).

From Travis Taylor: The time I felt like I wanted to be away from everyone was the time I was grounded and I did not do anything. I went to the place in the woods where I enjoy the most because it is just me and nature.

March 11

Dear Travis T,

   I feel like that sometimes too especially when you don't do anything to deserve it. When I get into this situation I just sit in my room and watch TV or do something to keep my mind off the trouble that I got into. Sometimes I do like you do—just get away from everybody and be by myself. Well, except my dog because he follows me everywhere. I also like to be alone in a quiet place where nobody is yelling at me or blaming me for anything.

Well, that is all I have to type, so until next time.

Sincerely,

Jennifer Lucas

Although Jennifer's first writing (in response to the Nikiski prompt) is a sincere effort to grapple with the issues at hand, it is written to the conference as a whole, without a specific reader in mind. It is also significant, I think, that she numbered her responses. Many of the prompts during all three years asked more than one question. It's interesting to me that many students organized their writing with numbers early in the conference, but this practice was virtually unseen later on. This type of writing was largely a new experience for students, whereas answering questions at the end of a story or poem in the literature anthology was old hat. As students explored this new form of discourse, many of them brought along the organization and expectations from the kinds of writing that were familiar to them in school. As they learned about their new audience and read examples of responses from other students, they had a better sense of the open-ended nature of the responses. I think this is what Phil Sittnick was referring to when he mentioned that students were letting go of the "right answer" pursuit.

Jennifer's responses clearly illustrate the emergence in the writer's mind of the specific reader. Her response to Travis would be interesting for all the participants, not only because it addresses a common theme, but also because Jennifer is writing to one person. The writing is focused and personal; Jennifer avoids addressing a world-at-large audience, a generic focus that tends to leave writing dull and colorless. I also have a sense that Jennifer had no real concern for a grade, or for the teacher's expectation for her second response. With the first response, she wanted to do what Phil had asked her to do, which was to answer the questions. In the second response she is writing back to another student to tell him what she thinks about his idea and experience; when she's done she says, "That's all I have to type." There is nothing artificial or contrived here.

Compare the processes that the students are actually engaged in and the things they are actually *doing* in this conference to the kinds of mindless, mass-produced busy work that fills so much of our students' days. This is a radical shift for traditional language arts classrooms. One of my favorite examples of such prescribed activities was from our district-mandated curriculum guide. In order to teach point of view, we were to ask our students to "imagine you are a dinner table, about to be set for a large meal." Imagine their excitement as they wrote those paragraphs! In the online conference setting, students are reading real, quality literature. They are thinking and discussing in open-ended terms not only the issues as they present themselves in the book, but also those that arrive from other classes. Students are determining their own audience and the content of their writing by selecting the prompts to respond to, and the students to address. They are responding as well as revising and editing their work with a real purpose, a real outlet for publication. Finally, they are celebrating their learning in a public and dynamic forum. This is not a flashy, new, cool thing to do with your students to impress the new technology director at the district office. This a quality learning activity based on sound principles of literacy learning.

Another Laguna student, Mandy Francis, also seems to have gone through a similar experience to Jennifer's. Her first response in the conference consists of two numbered replies that are performing or perfunctory in nature. Her second response is addressed to two specific students and addresses real issues in her personal life as they relate to the issue at hand.

Dear Students,

Hi! My name is Mandy Francis. I am in the eighth grade at Laguna Middle School. I am writing my response to the questions about the book ANNE FRANK.

1. Anne would like to be a young mature lady like her sister, Margot. This quote relates to my life a whole lot because I am beginning to act mature these days.

2. If I was coming out of hiding I would do all the stuff I didn't do before, like taking care of my family and helping people with needs.

My opinion of this book is that it is very interesting because Anne had an adventure of her life. She must have been real scared to be in that kind of situation. I know if I had been in her shoes I would probably freak out. Well I sure hope that doesn't happen around here, but we will never know.

Mandy Francis, Laguna, New Mexico

Dear Michelle Daniel and Renee Langley,

Hello! My name is Mandy Francis and I am in the 8th grade at Laguna Middle School. I like both of your images of a perfect mother because every mother should discipline and love you. My mother is the perfect mother because she is helpful and she always disciplines me when I say "I can't do this or that." She is like my best friend. I can talk to her all the time. She also teaches me what's right and what's wrong. I really love my mother a lot. Well, it was nice talking to both of you. I hope you write back. BYE!

Sincerely,

Mandy Francis

Although I sensed in the writing from Laguna more respect for parents than I saw in the writing from my students, it is still a risk for a student to say, "I really love my mother a lot," when it is clearly not fashionable for adolescents to claim parents as friends, as Mandy does. In thinking back to my experience in a native community, it's possible that this difference is cultural, reflecting closer ties between people in the home and in the community.

When Anne Frank writes "This 'self-consciousness' haunts me," she is referring to the most essential process in human development: becoming aware and self-critical of who we are and what we do. I hope that the one thing that jumped out at you as you read the previous samples of student writing is the emerging "self-consciousness" that Anne talked about. Whether they are writing about their mothers, their sisters, their communities, or themselves, students are making a straight-on effort to understand themselves and the world around them, and to articulate these insights and observations to others. In a curriculum guide or a lesson plan book, this process—free of education jargon—would read like this.

1. Read a good book.
2. As you read, discuss the issues as they arise.
3. As you read, write about these issues to others who are also reading the book.
4. Use technology as a tool to exchange your writing in a timely, organized manner.
5. Repeat as time allows.

Meaningful, sustained, purposeful discussions of literature with authentic audiences promote self-consciousness among students, not only in regard to their emerging consciousness as learners, but as people. Likewise, collaboration between teachers promotes the same sort of real, lasting change, a continually evolving self-consciousness that cannot be nurtured and fostered in isolation.

I'd like to close as we began, with a student's actual words from the Anne Frank Conference. I'd like to leave you with this question: Where, in the busy, often chaotic lives of our students, in the segmented, regimented, most institutionalized of experiences that is our public school system, can students reflect on their experience, share their views and their learning with others *about things that matter*, and leave with the sense of empowerment that this student expresses?

> Today growing up as a young black Christian girl has really had its ups and downs. I haven't had much said or done to me about what religion I am, but being a female, and black, I've had some bad days. Growing up in my family the boys get all of the "good

attention" and me, being a girl, I get the attention of "Don't come home with any babies. If you do, you will be taking care of them." Going to a school with the majority of the students being white, I've had some really trying experiences. But, I have learned how to cope with it from everyday life, and I plan to in the future.

Nikki Copeland, Guntown, Mississippi

Works Cited

Atwell, Nancie. 1987. *In the Middle: Writing, Reading, and Learning with Adolescents*. Upper Montclair, NJ: Boynton/Cook.

Berry, Wendell. 1985. "The Dream." In *The Collected Poems of Wendell Berry, 1957–1982*. San Francisco: North Point Press.

Carver, Raymond. 1993. "A Small, Good Thing." In *Short Cuts*. New York: Vintage.

D'Arcy, Pat. 1989. *Making Sense, Shaping Meaning: Writing in the Context of a Capacity-Based Approach to Learning*. Portsmouth: Boynton/Cook.

Fox, Mem. 1993. *Radical Reflections: Passionate Opinions on Teaching, Learning, and Living*. San Diego: Harcourt Brace.

Frank, Anne. 1942. *Anne Frank: The Diary of a Young Girl*. New York: Simon and Schuster.

Lee, Harper. [1960] 1995. *To Kill a Mockingbird*. Reprint. New York: HarperCollins.

Meir, Deborah. 1995. *The Power of Their Ideas: Lessons for America from a Small School in Harlem*. Boston: Beacon Press.

Moss, Beverly J., and Keith Walters. 1993. "Rethinking Diversity: Axes of Difference in the Writing Classroom" *Theory and Practice of Writing: Rethinking the Discipline*. Ed. Lee Odell. Carbondale: Southern Illinois University Press.

Rol, Ruud van der. 1993. *Anne Frank, Beyond the Diary: A Photographic Remembrance*. New York: Viking.

Royster, Jackie. 1996. "When the First Voice You Hear Is Not Your Own." *College Composition and Communication* 47.1: 29–40.

Taylor, Mildred D. 1991. *Roll of Thunder, Hear My Cry*. New York: Puffin Books.

Tierney, Robert J., and P. David Pearson. 1988. "Toward a Composing Model of Reading." In *Perspectives on Literacy*, Eds. Eugene R. Kintgen, Barry M. Kroll, and Mike Rose. Carbondale: Southern Illinois University Press.

Vygotsky, L. S. 1978. *Mind in Society: The Development of Higher Psychological Processes*. Eds. Michael Cole, Vera John-Steiner, Sylvia Scribner, and Ellen Souberman. Cambridge: Harvard University Press.

Yolen, Jane. 1988. *The Devil's Arithmetic*. New York: Viking Kestrel.

Index

Author

Scott Christian is currently an assistant professor at the University of Alaska—Southeast in Juneau. He is conducting two case studies focused on writing and portfolio assessment for the Spencer Foundation. He is also a research associate for the Harvard University Research and Documentation Project for the Annenberg Rural Challenge. He has been an active member of the Bread Loaf Rural Teacher Network for several years.

This book was set in Palatino and Helvetica.
Typefaces used on the cover were Univers and Monaco.
The book was printed on 60-lb., acid-free paper.